Gulf of Mexico Gumbo, page 24

Cooking Light

Soup

Oxmoor House

ISBN: 0-8487-3064-X
Library of Congress Control Number:
2006921188
Printed in the United States of America
First printing 2006

Be sure to check with your health-care provider
before making any changes in your diet.

Oxmoor House, Inc.
Editor in Chief: Nancy Fitzpatrick Wyatt
Executive Editor: Katherine M. Eakin
Copy Chief: Allison Long Lowery

Cooking Light® Soup
Editor: Heather Averett
Food Editors: Anne Cain, M.S., R.D.;
    Alyson Moreland Haynes
Copy Editor: Diane Rose
Editorial Assistants: Julie Boston,
    Brigette Gaucher
Photography Director: Jim Bathie
Senior Photo Stylist: Kay E. Clarke
Photo Stylist: Katherine Eckert
Director, Test Kitchens: Elizabeth Tyler Austin
Assistant Director, Test Kitchens:
    Julie Christopher
Test Kitchens Staff: Kristi Carter,
    Nicole Lee Faber, Kathleen Royal Phillips,
    Elise Weis, Kelley Self Wilton
Director of Production: Laura Lockhart
Publishing Systems Administrator: Rick Tucker
Production Manager: Greg A. Amason
Production Assistant: Faye Porter Bonner

Contributors:
Designer: Carol Damsky
Indexer: Mary Ann Laurens
Editorial Interns: Rachel Quinlivan, R.D.;
    Mary Catherine Shamblin;
    Vanessa Rusch Thomas; Ashley Wells
Photographers: Beau Gustafson, Lee Harrelson
Photo Stylist: Lydia DeGaris-Pursell

To order additional publications, call
1-800-765-6400, or visit oxmoorhouse.com

CONTENTS

Essential Soups 8

From zesty chili to chunky chowder,
here are the best of the traditional
soups. When you crave that familiar
bowl of comfort like your mother
made, here are the new *Cooking Light*
classics—as good as ever but better
for you.

Appetizer & Dessert Soups 36

Sweet or savory, hot or cold, choose
soup for a delicious beginning or end to
a great meal. Try a zippy gazpacho or a
creamy vichyssoise as an appetizer,
or serve a cool fruit soup for a surprising
and irresistible dessert.

Smooth & Creamy Soups 56

For pure flavor and pleasurable mouth
feel with every spoonful, select from
these velvety concoctions. It's hard to
beat basic cream of asparagus, but we
go a step further by offering more
intriguing medleys, such as tomato soup
spiked with balsamic vinegar.

Quick & Easy Soups 74

Go for quick comfort with these simply sensational soups, perfected for fast preparation and incredible flavor. From a rustic chicken stew to a hearty bean soup, these are the ones we turn to when we want healthy homemade soups in a hurry.

Hearty Soups & Stews 92

Juicy chunks of meat, rich broths, and bright seasonings—nothing beats the satisfying depths of these robust recipes. For a wintry evening stew, choose from our best beef or lamb recipes, or select a divine sausage, barley, and mushroom masterpiece.

Melting Pot   110

Could world peace be achieved with soup? Everyone everywhere loves this dish. From famed French onion soup to a hot and sour soup that's better than any restaurant version, experience a spicy world of cuisines, each distinguished by unique ingredient combos.

Cooking Light®
Editor in Chief: Mary Kay Culpepper
Executive Editor: Billy R. Sims
Art Director: Susan Waldrip Dendy
Managing Editor: Maelynn Cheung
Senior Food Editor: Alison Mann Ashton
Senior Editor: Anamary Pelayo
Features Editor: Phillip Rhodes
Projects Editor: Mary Simpson Creel, M.S., R.D.
Associate Food Editors: Timothy Q. Cebula,
    Ann Taylor Pittman
Assistant Food Editor: Kathy C. Kitchens, R.D.
Assistant Editor: Cindy Hatcher
Contributing Beauty Editor: Carol Straley
Test Kitchens Director: Vanessa Taylor Johnson
Food Stylist: Kellie Gerber Kelley
Assistant Food Stylist: M. Kathleen Kanen
Test Kitchens Professionals: Sam Brannock,
    Kathryn Conrad, Mary H. Drennen,
    Jan Jacks Moon, Tiffany Vickers,
    Mike Wilson
Assistant Art Director: Maya Metz Logue
Senior Designers: Fernande Bondarenko,
    J. Shay McNamee
Designer: Brigette Mayer
Senior Photographers: Becky Luigart-Stayner,
    Randy Mayor
Senior Photo Stylist: Cindy Barr
Photo Stylists: Melanie J. Clarke, Jan Gautro
Digital Photo Stylist: Jan A. Smith
Studio Assistant: Celine Chenoweth
Copy Chief: Maria Parker Hopkins
Senior Copy Editor: Susan Roberts
Copy Editor: Johannah Paiva
Production Manager: Liz Rhoades
Production Editors: Joanne McCrary Brasseal,
    Hazel R. Eddins
Administrative Coordinator: Carol D. Johnson
Office Manager: Rita K. Jackson
Editorial Assistants: Melissa Hoover,
    Brandy Rushing
Correspondence Editor: Michelle Gibson Daniels
Interns: Rachel Cardina, Marie Hegler,
    Emily Self

CookingLight.com
Editor: Jennifer Middleton Richards
Online Producer: Abigail Masters

Cover: *Baked Potato and Bacon Soup* (page 20)

Welcome

Soup is adaptable, dependable, and just plain enjoyable. But there's another thing that soup is, and that's essential. For a *Cooking Light*® cook, soup is grace for the table.

In this cookbook, you'll find the soup recipes we at *Cooking Light* believe to be the essential recipes for every *Cooking Light* cook. These recipes are our tried-and-true classics—ones we love to make again and again.

Each chapter offers mouthwatering, flavorful recipes, complete with nutritional analyses that will help you to eat smart, be fit, and live well. After all, eating smart, being fit, and living well are essential in our minds.

So whether you're looking for a down-home recipe for Turkey Noodle Soup or for something a little more upscale, such as Cream of Asparagus Soup, you're sure to find it in this edition of *The Cooking Light Cook's Essential Recipe Collection*. It's my sincere hope that these recipes will become as essential to your family as they are to the *Cooking Light* family.

Very truly yours,

Mary Kay Culpepper
Editor in Chief

essential
soups

Tomato-Basil Soup

Slicing into thin strips (making a chiffonade) is a good technique for herbs such as basil or for any large-leafed vegetable, such as spinach or lettuce. Start by neatly stacking four to five leaves and tightly rolling them. Use a chef's knife to slice across the roll to produce strips or ribbons.

2 teaspoons olive oil
3 garlic cloves, minced
3 cups fat-free, less-sodium chicken broth
¾ teaspoon salt
3 (14.5-ounce) cans no salt–added diced tomatoes, undrained
2 cups fresh basil leaves, thinly sliced
Whole basil leaves or chiffonade (optional)

1. Heat oil in a large saucepan over medium heat. Add garlic; cook 30 seconds, stirring constantly. Stir in broth, salt, and tomatoes; bring to a boil. Reduce heat; simmer 20 minutes. Stir in sliced basil.
2. Place half of soup in a blender; process until smooth. Pour puréed soup into a bowl; repeat procedure with remaining soup. Ladle soup into individual bowls. Garnish with whole basil leaves, if desired. Yield: 4 servings (serving size: 1½ cups).

CALORIES 103 (24% from fat); FAT 2.8g (sat 0.4g, mono 1.7g, poly 0.4g); PROTEIN 5.8g; CARB 15.9g; FIBER 4g; CHOL 0mg; IRON 2.4mg; SODIUM 809mg; CALC 129mg

No one will ever guess that the base for this soup is canned tomatoes. Basil and tomatoes are perfect partners, but in this recipe, fresh basil takes the lead. It transforms an ordinary can of tomatoes into a refreshing soup chock-full of vine-ripened tomato flavor.

Broccoli and Cheese Soup

Cooking spray
- 1 cup chopped onion
- 2 garlic cloves, minced
- 3 cups fat-free, less-sodium chicken broth
- 1 (16-ounce) package broccoli florets
- ⅓ cup all-purpose flour
- 2½ cups 2% reduced-fat milk
- ¼ teaspoon black pepper
- 8 ounces light processed cheese, cubed (such as Velveeta Light)

1. Heat a large nonstick saucepan over medium-high heat. Coat pan with cooking spray. Add onion and garlic; sauté 3 minutes or until tender. Add broth and broccoli. Bring broccoli mixture to a boil over medium-high heat. Reduce heat to medium; cook 10 minutes.

2. Lightly spoon flour into a dry measuring cup; level with a knife. Combine milk and flour, stirring with a whisk until well blended; add to broccoli mixture. Cook 5 minutes or until slightly thick, stirring constantly. Stir in pepper. Remove from heat; add cheese, stirring until cheese melts.

3. Place one-third of soup in a blender or food processor; process until smooth. Return puréed soup to pan. Yield: 6 servings (serving size: 1⅓ cups).

CALORIES 203 (28% from fat); FAT 6.3g (sat 4g, mono 1.8g, poly 0.4g); PROTEIN 15.6g; CARB 21.7g; FIBER 2.9g; CHOL 24mg; IRON 1.2mg; SODIUM 897mg; CALC 385mg

Although nothing can compare to the distinctive flavor of natural cheeses, sometimes processed cheese is the best choice. Processed cheese products are created when two or more natural cheeses are combined with other ingredients, such as nonfat milk solids, cream or butter, and water. American cheese and Velveeta are examples. They retain the flavor of natural cheese but have a longer storage life, and they melt smoothly to create a velvety texture. Light processed cheese contains about 50 percent less fat and 25 percent fewer calories than the original, but it still adds rich, creamy cheese flavor.

Just about every seasoned cook and every restaurant menu has a recipe for broccoli and cheese soup. It pairs perfectly with a ham or turkey sandwich for lunch or a light dinner. In our version, we use processed cheese, which melts beautifully, giving this soup a smooth texture and a mild flavor. A baked potato and broiled tomatoes topped with Italian-herbed seasoning and mozzarella round out the meal.

Split Pea Soup with Rosemary

Split peas come from a variety of green and yellow peas that are specifically grown for drying. Once dried, the peas are steamed to loosen their skins. The skins are removed and the peas are split along a natural seam. Both green and yellow varieties are as nutritious as dried beans, but unlike dried beans, they do not need a long soak before cooking, and they require a shorter cook time. Yellow peas have a slightly sweeter flavor than that of the earthier green. Both varieties can be found in supermarkets and health-food stores and are usually sold in 1-pound plastic bags.

1½ cups green split peas
2 teaspoons olive oil, divided
2 cups chopped onion
1 cup diced carrot
1 bay leaf
1 tablespoon minced garlic cloves, divided
1 tablespoon minced fresh rosemary, divided
1 teaspoon paprika
¼ teaspoon black pepper
1 tablespoon tomato paste
1 tablespoon low-sodium soy sauce
4 cups water
1 (14-ounce) can vegetable broth
¼ cup chopped fresh parsley, divided
¼ cup reduced-fat sour cream

1. Sort and wash peas. Place peas in a saucepan. Cover with water to 2 inches above peas; set aside. Heat 1 teaspoon oil in a Dutch oven over medium-high heat. Add onion, carrot, and bay leaf, and sauté 5 minutes, stirring frequently. Add 2 teaspoons garlic, 1 teaspoon rosemary, paprika, and pepper; cook 3 minutes. Add tomato paste and soy sauce, and cook until liquid evaporates, scraping pan to loosen browned bits.

2. Drain peas. Add peas, 4 cups water, and broth to onion mixture; bring to a boil. Cover, reduce heat to medium-low, and simmer 1 hour, stirring often. Discard bay leaf. Place half of soup in a blender or food processor; process until smooth. Pour puréed soup into a bowl. Repeat procedure with remaining soup.

3. Combine remaining 1 teaspoon oil, remaining 1 teaspoon garlic, remaining 2 teaspoons rosemary, and 3 tablespoons parsley; stir into soup. Ladle soup into individual bowls; top each serving with sour cream and remaining 1 tablespoon parsley. Yield: 6 servings (serving size: about 1 cup soup, 2 teaspoons sour cream and ½ teaspoon parsley).

CALORIES 249 (10% from fat); FAT 2.9g (sat 1g, mono 1.1g, poly 0.2g); PROTEIN 14.4g; CARB 42.6g; FIBER 1.8g; CHOL 5mg; IRON 2.3mg; SODIUM 299mg; CALC 43mg

This is a unique and tasty variation of split pea soup. Hearty enough for dinner, it also keeps well in the refrigerator. Try serving it with whole-grain bread.

Wild Rice and Mushroom Soup

Wild rice can almost be considered a perfect ingredient for soup. Unlike regular rice that can get soft and mushy when cooked too long, wild rice maintains its chewy texture. It adds a rich, nutty flavor and is a great source of fiber. For best results, use 100 percent wild rice, and cook it until the grains start to split (a sign that the rice is tender enough to eat). The brand you use isn't important as long as the label indicates that it's 100 percent wild rice and not a blend.

2 teaspoons butter
½ cup chopped carrot (about 1 medium carrot)
1 large onion, chopped
2 celery stalks, thinly sliced (about ¾ cup)
1 (8-ounce) package presliced mushrooms
1 teaspoon chopped fresh or ¼ teaspoon dried rosemary
¼ teaspoon black pepper
3 garlic cloves, minced
2 (14-ounce) cans fat-free, less-sodium chicken broth
1 cup uncooked wild rice
⅓ cup all-purpose flour
2¾ cups 2% reduced-fat milk
2 tablespoons dry sherry
¾ teaspoon salt

1. Melt butter in a Dutch oven over medium-high heat. Add carrot and next 6 ingredients; sauté 8 minutes or until tender. Stir in broth, scraping pan to loosen browned bits. Stir in rice; bring to a boil. Cover, reduce heat, and simmer 1 hour and 15 minutes or until rice is tender.
2. Lightly spoon flour into a dry measuring cup; level with a knife. Combine flour and milk in a small bowl, stirring with a whisk. Add to soup mixture. Cook over medium heat 10 minutes or until thick, stirring frequently. Stir in sherry and salt. Yield: 8 servings (serving size: 1 cup).

CALORIES 185 (15% from fat); FAT 3g (sat 1.5g, mono 0.9g, poly 0.1g); PROTEIN 8.6g; CARB 30.1g; FIBER 1.7g; CHOL 8.8mg; IRON 0.9mg; SODIUM 557mg; CALC 119mg

Simple elegance—that's how to best describe this soup. It offers all the warmth and heartiness of a vegetable or beef soup, yet it's fancy enough to serve as a starter at a dinner party. A splash of sherry adds a little richness that will make you and your guests think there's cream in the soup, but it's actually reduced-fat milk.

Garden Minestrone

The key to perfectly cooked vegetables starts before you ever add heat. Chopping or slicing vegetables the same size or thickness will ensure that they cook evenly. This is particularly important for carrots, potatoes, and other vegetables with longer cook times. If you're in a hurry, remember that the smaller the chop or the thinner the slice, the shorter the cook time.

2 teaspoons olive oil
1 cup chopped onion
2 teaspoons chopped fresh oregano
4 garlic cloves, minced
3 cups chopped yellow squash
3 cups chopped zucchini
1 cup chopped carrot
1 cup fresh corn kernels (about 2 ears)
4 cups chopped tomato, divided
3 (14-ounce) cans fat-free, less-sodium chicken broth
½ cup uncooked ditalini (very short tube-shaped macaroni)
1 (15.5-ounce) can Great Northern beans, rinsed and drained
1 (6-ounce) package fresh baby spinach
1 teaspoon salt
½ teaspoon freshly ground black pepper
1 cup (4 ounces) grated Asiago cheese
Coarsely ground black pepper (optional)

1. Heat oil in a Dutch oven over medium-high heat. Add chopped onion to pan, and sauté 3 minutes or until softened. Add oregano and garlic, and sauté 1 minute. Stir in squash, zucchini, carrot, and corn; sauté 5 minutes or until vegetables are tender. Remove from heat.

2. Place 3 cups tomato and 1 can broth in a blender; process until smooth. Add tomato mixture to pan; return pan to heat. Stir in remaining 1 cup tomato and 2 cans broth; bring mixture to a boil. Reduce heat, and simmer 20 minutes.

3. Add pasta and beans to pan, and cook 10 minutes or until pasta is tender, stirring occasionally. Remove from heat. Stir in spinach, salt, and ½ teaspoon freshly ground pepper. Ladle soup into individual bowls; top with cheese. Garnish with coarsely ground pepper, if desired. Yield: 8 servings (serving size: 1½ cups soup and 2 tablespoons cheese).

CALORIES 217 (25% from fat); FAT 6.1g (sat 2.7g, mono 2g, poly 0.6g); PROTEIN 12.6g; CARB 30.5g; FIBER 7.9g; CHOL 12mg; IRON 2.7mg; SODIUM 812mg; CALC 206mg

An adaptation of the classic Italian minestra, this recipe is full of late-summer produce: tomatoes, squash, fresh spinach, corn, and carrots. In cooler months, use peeled acorn squash and Swiss chard in place of squash and spinach. We love this minestrone for its practicality, since it's convenient for lunch or a simple dinner (just serve it with a tossed green salad and some crusty bread).

Baked Potato and Bacon Soup

While the microwave may be the fastest way to "bake" a potato, a hot oven produces the best flavor. Oven-baking will yield a potato that's crisp on the outside and white and fluffy within. Russet potatoes, with their slightly mealy texture, are recommended for baking over other varieties that have a waxy texture. For this recipe, the skins get mashed with the rest of the potato, contributing to the overall flavor and texture.

5¼ pounds baking potatoes
7 bacon slices
4½ cups chopped onion
1 teaspoon salt
5 garlic cloves, minced
1 bay leaf
7½ cups 1% low-fat milk
¾ teaspoon black pepper
3 cups fat-free, less-sodium chicken broth
⅓ cup chopped fresh parsley (optional)
1¼ cups sliced green onions
1¼ cups (5 ounces) finely shredded reduced-fat sharp Cheddar cheese

1. Preheat oven to 400°.
2. Pierce potatoes with a fork; bake at 400° for 1 hour or until tender. Cool slightly. Partially mash potatoes, including skins, with a potato masher; set aside.
3. Cook bacon in a Dutch oven over medium heat until crisp. Remove bacon from pan; crumble, and set aside. Add onion to bacon drippings in pan; sauté 5 minutes. Add salt, garlic, and bay leaf; sauté 2 minutes. Add potato, milk, pepper, and broth; bring to a boil. Reduce heat; simmer 10 minutes. Stir in parsley, if desired. Ladle soup into individual bowls; top with bacon, green onions, and cheese. Yield: 18 servings (serving size: 1 cup soup, about 1 teaspoon bacon, about 1 tablespoon green onions, and about 1 tablespoon cheese).

CALORIES 237 (30% from fat); FAT 7.8g (sat 3.5g, mono 3.1g, poly 0.8g); PROTEIN 10.5g; CARB 31.8g; FIBER 3.1g; CHOL 15mg; IRON 2mg; SODIUM 394mg; CALC 228mg

You're probably familiar with this popular restaurant selection made with heavy cream and loaded with toppings. Our version has all the flavor but with far less fat and fewer calories. This recipe serves a crowd, which makes it a great choice for casual get-togethers. But it can easily be cut in half. To simplify the preparation, bake the potatoes and shred the cheese the day before making the soup. If the soup needs to simmer for a while on the stove, you may need to add more chicken broth to keep it from getting too thick.

(pictured on cover)

Creamy Lentil Soup

3 bacon slices
2 cups chopped leek
1 cup chopped onion
3 cups water
2 cups chopped peeled
  baking potato
1 cup dried lentils
¾ cup chopped carrot
½ teaspoon salt
1 (14-ounce) can fat-free,
  less-sodium chicken broth
½ cup half-and-half
1 tablespoon dry sherry
Fresh flat-leaf parsley sprigs
  (optional)

1. Cook bacon in a Dutch oven over medium heat until crisp. Remove bacon from pan, reserving drippings in pan. Crumble bacon; set aside.

2. Add leek and onion to pan; sauté 4 minutes. Add water, potato, lentils, carrot, salt, and broth; bring to a boil. Cover, reduce heat, and simmer 1 hour or until vegetables are tender.

3. Place in a blender or food processor; process until smooth. Return puréed mixture to pan; stir in half-and-half and sherry. Cook until thoroughly heated. Ladle soup into individual bowls. Sprinkle with bacon. Garnish with parsley sprigs, if desired. Yield: 6 servings (serving size: 1⅓ cups).

CALORIES 287 (29% from fat); FAT 9.4g (sat 4g, mono 3.7g, poly 1.1g); PROTEIN 13.6g; CARB 37.4g; FIBER 5.8g; CHOL 15mg; IRON 4.2mg; SODIUM 465mg; CALC 72mg

With 25 percent protein, lentils have one of the highest protein levels of any vegetable, and they are often used as a staple in many countries with large vegetarian populations, such as India. Lentils can be found in different sizes and colors, ranging from yellow to red-orange to green and brown, all of which can be purchased whole or split. But the most common varieties found in U.S. supermarkets are brown and green. Lentils cook quickly and don't require soaking, as other dried legumes do. They lend mild, nutty flavor that melds well with a wide variety of ingredients.

Half-and-half adds creamy body and a satiny finish to this hearty soup. Serve with breadsticks and a salad for a simple, yet filling, supper. Make this a vegetarian soup by substituting 2 tablespoons canola oil for the bacon drippings and vegetable broth for the chicken broth.

Gulf of Mexico Gumbo

For portion control and to transform an ordinary serving of gumbo into a dish that is picture-perfect, try this trick. Instead of spooning rice into an individual serving bowl, lightly pack ½ cup of hot cooked rice into a custard cup or dry measuring cup. Then invert the cup of rice into the center of the bowl, and ladle the gumbo or soup around the rice.

1 cup all-purpose flour
1 teaspoon canola oil
2 cups chopped onion
1 cup chopped green bell pepper
½ cup chopped celery
4 garlic cloves, minced
1 cup sliced okra
1 cup chopped tomato
1½ cups water
1 teaspoon Cajun-Creole Seasoning
4 (8-ounce) bottles clam juice
2 bay leaves
½ pound skinless red snapper or other firm white fish fillet, cut into 1-inch pieces
¼ cup thinly sliced green onions
¾ pound crawfish, peeled
¼ pound medium shrimp, peeled and deveined
½ teaspoon hot sauce
4½ cups hot cooked long-grain rice

1. Lightly spoon flour into a dry measuring cup; level with a knife. Place flour in a 9-inch cast-iron skillet, and cook over medium heat 10 minutes or until browned, stirring constantly with a whisk (if flour browns too fast, remove from heat, and stir constantly until flour cools). Remove from heat; set aside.
2. Heat oil in a large Dutch oven over medium heat. Add onion, bell pepper, celery, and garlic; sauté 8 minutes or until tender. Add okra and tomato. Cover; cook 5 minutes, stirring occasionally. Add 1½ cups water, Cajun-Creole Seasoning, clam juice, and bay leaves; bring to a boil. Gradually add browned flour, stirring with a whisk. Reduce heat; simmer, uncovered, 45 minutes, stirring occasionally.
3. Add snapper; cook 5 minutes. Add green onions, crawfish, and shrimp; cook 10 minutes or until seafood is done. Stir in hot sauce; discard bay leaves. Serve over rice. Yield: 9 servings (serving size: 1 cup gumbo and ½ cup rice).

(Totals include Cajun-Creole Seasoning) CALORIES 251 (6% from fat); FAT 1.8g (sat 0.3g, mono 0.6g, poly 0.6g); PROTEIN 17.8g; CARB 39.8g; FIBER 2.3g; CHOL 71mg; IRON 2.8mg; SODIUM 460mg; CALC 72mg

Cajun-Creole Seasoning

1 tablespoon salt
¾ teaspoon ground red pepper
½ teaspoon garlic powder
½ teaspoon black pepper

1. Combine all ingredients. Yield: about 1½ tablespoons.

Most Cajuns agree that the secret to the best gumbo is the roux, a mixture of equal parts flour and oil cooked over low heat until the mixture turns a rich coppery brown. Our secret to an almost fat-free version of this traditional dish is to slowly brown the flour without the oil in a cast-iron skillet.

New England Clam Chowder

Canned clams are ideal for recipes that call for only the meat of the clams. You can buy them whole or chopped. Be aware that, as with most canned products, canned clams are higher in sodium than fresh. Clam juice, the strained liquid of shucked clams, is often used as a cooking liquid for seafood dishes. It has a briny flavor and can be found in most grocery stores.

2 (6½-ounce) cans minced clams, undrained
Cooking spray
1 cup chopped onion
2 turkey-bacon slices, chopped
1 garlic clove, minced
3 cups chopped peeled red potato (about 1¼ pounds)
½ teaspoon dried thyme
2 (8-ounce) bottles clam juice
3 tablespoons all-purpose flour
2½ cups 2% low-fat milk
Freshly ground black pepper
Fresh thyme sprigs (optional)

1. Drain clams, reserving liquid; set clams and liquid aside. Heat a Dutch oven over medium heat. Coat pan with cooking spray. Add onion, bacon slices, and garlic; sauté 5 minutes. Add reserved clam liquid, potato, thyme, and clam juice; bring mixture to a boil. Cover, reduce heat, and simmer 20 minutes or until potato is tender.

2. Place 2 cups potato mixture, including bacon, in a blender, and process until smooth. Add potato purée to potato mixture in Dutch oven; stir well. Combine flour and milk, stirring with a wire whisk until blended; add to chowder. Cook over medium heat, stirring constantly, 10 minutes or until thickened. Stir in clams. Ladle soup into individual bowls, and sprinkle with pepper. Garnish with thyme, if desired. Yield: 6¾ cups (serving size: 1 cup).

CALORIES 163 (15% from fat); FAT 2.8g (sat 1.4g, mono 0.5g, poly 0.1g); PROTEIN 9.7g; CARB 24.9g; FIBER 1.9g; CHOL 22mg; IRON 1.8mg; SODIUM 473mg; CALC 135mg

There are two well-known styles of clam chowder— Manhattan and New England. New England–style is definitely the most common. Known for its creamy, white milk-base loaded with tiny, chewy clams and starchy, hearty potatoes, New England clam chowder graces the table in homes and restaurants all across the country, not just along the eastern seaboard. Manhattan-style chowder, however, is a tomato-based dish and is most popular, of course, in New York.

All-American Chili

Cooking with wine adds depth of flavor to any dish or sauce. In this recipe, fruity red wine balances the bold and spicy ingredients for maximum impact. Adding the wine early in the cooking process allows it to blend with the seasonings. During cooking, most of the alcohol evaporates, intensifying the flavor. While the wine you cook with doesn't have to be expensive, it needs to be of a good quality because it contributes so much to the final dish. Cooking wines aren't recommended because they have salt and food coloring added, and they usually have an inferior flavor.

6 ounces hot turkey Italian sausage
2 cups chopped onion
1 cup chopped green bell pepper
8 garlic cloves, minced
1 pound ground sirloin
1 jalapeño pepper, chopped
3 tablespoons tomato paste
2 tablespoons chili powder
2 tablespoons brown sugar
1 tablespoon ground cumin
1 teaspoon dried oregano
½ teaspoon freshly ground black pepper
¼ teaspoon salt
2 bay leaves
1¼ cups merlot or other fruity red wine
2 (28-ounce) cans whole tomatoes, undrained and coarsely chopped
2 (15-ounce) cans kidney beans, rinsed and drained

1. Heat a large Dutch oven over medium-high heat. Remove casings from sausage. Add sausage, onion, and next 4 ingredients to pan; cook 8 minutes or until sausage and beef are browned, stirring to crumble.

2. Add tomato paste and next 7 ingredients, and cook 1 minute, stirring constantly. Stir in wine, tomatoes, and kidney beans, and bring to a boil. Cover, reduce heat, and simmer 1 hour, stirring occasionally.

3. Uncover and cook 30 minutes, stirring occasionally. Discard bay leaves. Ladle soup into individual bowls. Yield: 8 servings (serving size: 1¼ cups chili).

CALORIES 239 (20% from fat); FAT 5.4g (sat 1.8g, mono 1.6g, poly 0.9g); PROTEIN 20.4g; CARB 29.9g; FIBER 7.9g; CHOL 41mg; IRON 6.7mg; SODIUM 736mg; CALC 119mg

From college football's spirited tailgates to extravaganzas celebrating the Super Bowl, a warm, spicy bowl of chili is just the ticket for game-day success. No gridiron spread is complete without it.

Tex-Mex Chicken Tortilla Soup

The hottest parts of a pepper are the seeds and membrane, so if you want to reduce the heat in a dish, remove the seeds. When cutting or seeding hot peppers, wear rubber gloves to prevent hands from being burned. To seed the peppers, slice off the stem end, and cut the pepper in half lengthwise. Remove the seeds by running your finger along the inside of the vein, scraping off the seeds. Stack the two pepper halves on top of each other, and cut into irregular pieces about the size of peas.

1 tablespoon olive oil
2 (6-ounce) skinless, boneless chicken breast halves, cut into ½-inch pieces
2 (4-ounce) skinless, boneless chicken thighs, cut into ½-inch pieces
2 cups chopped onion (about 2 medium)
3 garlic cloves, chopped
1 cup fresh corn kernels (about 2 ears) or frozen whole-kernel corn
1 cup water
1 tablespoon chopped jalapeño pepper
1 tablespoon chili powder
1½ teaspoons ground cumin
½ teaspoon salt
2 (14.5-ounce) cans no salt–added tomatoes, undrained and chopped
2 (14-ounce) cans fat-free, less-sodium chicken broth
1 (4.5-ounce) can chopped green chiles
2 (6-inch) corn tortillas, each cut into 8 wedges
5 tablespoons reduced-fat sour cream
Cilantro sprigs (optional)

1. Heat olive oil in a large Dutch oven over medium-high heat. Add chicken pieces and chopped onion, and cook 7 minutes or until onion is tender. Add chopped garlic to pan, and sauté 30 seconds. Stir in corn and next 8 ingredients. Bring to a boil, reduce heat, and simmer 45 minutes.
2. Preheat oven to 350°.
3. Place tortilla wedges on baking sheet, and bake at 350° for 5 minutes or until crisp.
4. Ladle soup into individual bowls, and top with sour cream. Garnish with tortilla chips and cilantro sprigs, if desired. Yield: 5 servings (serving size: 1½ cups soup, 1 tablespoon sour cream, and about 3 tortilla chips).

CALORIES 331 (27% from fat); FAT 9.9g (sat 2.8g, mono 3.6g, poly 1.4g); PROTEIN 30.6g; CARB 30.9g; FIBER 6.1g; CHOL 77mg; IRON 2.3mg; SODIUM 983mg; CALC 130mg

Tortillas are the basis of countless Mexican dishes, such as tacos, enchiladas, and burritos, as well as for our peppy Tex-Mex soup. The crunchy texture of the tortilla chips provides the perfect contrast to this fiesta-in-a-bowl, which features bright colors, bold flavors, robust spices, and sour cream and cilantro garnishes. Don't throw away any leftover tortillas; they're also ideal toasted and sprinkled over salads or casseroles.

Brunswick Stew with Smoked Paprika

Dried over smoldering oak logs, Spanish paprika has a strong, smoky flavor. And the aroma is deep, intense, sweet, and spicy. The color is a striking deep red that spreads through any dish to which it is added.

2 cups (¾-inch) cubed Yukon gold potato
2 cups thinly sliced yellow onion
2 cups frozen corn kernels, thawed
1 cup frozen baby lima beans, thawed
½ cup tomato sauce
2 (14-ounce) cans fat-free, less-sodium chicken broth
2 bacon slices, cut crosswise into ½-inch strips
3 cups shredded cooked chicken breast
½ teaspoon sweet Spanish smoked paprika
½ teaspoon kosher salt
¼ teaspoon ground red pepper
Coarsely ground black pepper (optional)

1. Combine first 7 ingredients in a Dutch oven over medium-high heat; bring to a boil. Reduce heat to low; simmer 30 minutes or until potatoes are tender, stirring occasionally. Stir in chicken and next 3 ingredients; simmer 15 minutes. Ladle stew into individual bowls. Sprinkle with coarsely ground black pepper, if desired. Yield: 6 servings (serving size: about 1½ cups).

CALORIES 308 (22% from fat); FAT 7.5g (sat 2.4g, mono 3g, poly 1.4g); PROTEIN 29.4g; CARB 31.6g; FIBER 4.9g; CHOL 65mg; IRON 2.2mg; SODIUM 645mg; CALC 36mg

This recipe is said to have originated in Brunswick County, Virginia, in the 1800s. We spiced it up with a little Spanish smoked paprika (available at gourmet specialty stores and some supermarkets). Use rotisserie chicken to speed up preparation. This hearty stew could become a regular autumn weeknight treat.

Turkey Noodle Soup

To chop an onion, cut onion in half lengthwise (stem end to root), and remove the papery skin. Place each half, cut side down, on a cutting board, and make several parallel horizontal cuts almost to the root end. Then make several parallel vertical cuts through the onion layers, but again, don't cut through the root end. Finally, cut across the grain to make chopped pieces. To chop celery, place a celery stalk, curved side up, on a cutting board. Make two to three cuts along the length of the stalk, and then cut across to make chopped pieces. What you'll get are perfect-sized vegetables to toss in your soup.

Cooking spray
1 cup (¼-inch-thick) slices carrot
¾ cup chopped onion
4 garlic cloves, minced
1 cup (¼-inch-thick) slices celery
¼ teaspoon salt
¼ teaspoon freshly ground black pepper
6 cups fat-free, less-sodium chicken broth
2 cups (3 ounces) uncooked egg noodles
1 tablespoon low-sodium soy sauce
1 bay leaf
2 cups shredded cooked turkey (about 8 ounces)
Coarsely ground black pepper (optional)

1. Heat a large saucepan over medium-high heat. Coat pan with cooking spray. Add carrot, onion, and garlic, and sauté 5 minutes or until onion is lightly browned. Add celery, salt, and ¼ teaspoon pepper, and sauté 3 minutes. Add broth and next 3 ingredients; bring to a boil. Reduce heat, and simmer 5 minutes. Add turkey; cook 3 minutes. Discard bay leaf. Ladle soup into individual bowls. Sprinkle with coarsely ground pepper, if desired. Yield: 4 servings (serving size: 2 cups).

CALORIES 280 (23% from fat); FAT 7.2g (sat 2.6g, mono 1.1g, poly 1.4g); PROTEIN 29.1g; CARB 24.3g; FIBER 2.3g; CHOL 80mg; IRON 2.6mg; SODIUM 544mg; CALC 79mg

Chicken noodle soup provides that all-encompassing layer of comfort that only it (and a mother) can provide. Now that you're all grown up, try this turkey variation of your childhood favorite. You can also enjoy this soup with shredded chicken instead of turkey if you'd prefer.

appetizer & dessert soups

Gazpacho with Avocado and Cumin Chips

Here are the steps to follow to peel and seed an avocado: Cut into the avocado all the way around using a sharp knife. You'll hit the large seed in the center, so don't expect to be able to cut all the way through the fruit. Once you've cut around it, twist both sides, and pull the halves apart. Take the knife and whack the seed; pull to remove the seed, which will be stuck on the knife blade. Using a spoon, gently scoop the flesh of the avocado from the shell.

1½ cups bottled Bloody Mary mix (such as Major Peters')
1½ cups finely diced tomato
1 cup finely diced yellow bell pepper
¾ cup chopped seeded peeled cucumber
¾ cup finely diced red onion
2 tablespoons fresh lime juice
1 teaspoon red wine vinegar
1 teaspoon Worcestershire sauce
½ teaspoon freshly ground black pepper
2 garlic cloves, crushed
1 (5.5-ounce) can low-sodium vegetable juice
1 (5.5-ounce) can tomato juice
¾ cup diced peeled avocado
¾ cup chopped green onions
Cumin Chips

1. Combine first 12 ingredients in a large nonaluminum bowl. Cover and chill. Ladle soup into individual bowls; sprinkle with avocado and green onions. Serve with Cumin Chips. Yield: 6 servings (serving size: 1 cup soup, 2 tablespoons avocado, 2 tablespoons green onions, and 4 Cumin Chips).

(Totals include Cumin Chips) CALORIES 129 (27% from fat); FAT 3.8g (sat 0.6g, mono 2g, poly 0.7g); PROTEIN 3g; CARB 22.8g; FIBER 3.4g; CHOL 0mg; IRON 2mg; SODIUM 571mg; CALC 75mg

Cumin Chips

4 (6-inch) corn tortillas, each cut into 6 wedges
Cooking spray
½ teaspoon ground cumin

1. Preheat oven to 350°.
2. Place tortilla wedges on a large baking sheet. Lightly coat wedges with cooking spray, and sprinkle with cumin. Bake at 350° for 10 minutes or until chips are lightly browned and crisp. Yield: 2 dozen (serving size: 4 chips).

Traditionally, gazpacho is a cold, uncooked Spanish soup made of fresh tomatoes, bell peppers, onions, and cucumbers and often garnished with croutons. Cumin chips and avocado stand in for the croutons here, giving it additional Spanish flair. If you're making gazpacho in the summer, you'll find many wonderful tomato varieties to choose from. In the winter, try using plum tomatoes, which have a meaty flesh that holds up well in soup.

Cool Summer-Berry Soup

2 cups fresh raspberries
2 cups halved fresh
    strawberries
½ cup cranberry-raspberry
    juice drink
½ cup dry white wine
¼ cup sugar
⅛ teaspoon ground cinnamon
1 (6-ounce) carton strawberry
    low-fat yogurt
Reduced-fat sour cream
    (optional)

1. To prepare soup, place first 3 ingredients in a blender; process until smooth. Strain berry mixture through a sieve into a medium saucepan. Stir in wine, sugar, and cinnamon, and bring to a boil over medium heat. Cook 2 minutes; remove from heat. Place in a large bowl; cover and chill 3 hours. Stir in yogurt.

2. Ladle 1 cup soup into each of 4 individual bowls. Garnish with reduced-fat sour cream, if desired. Yield: 4 servings.

CALORIES 172 (5% from fat); FAT 1g (sat 0.3g, mono 0.1g, poly 0.4g); PROTEIN 2.6g; CARB 40.2g; FIBER 5.7g; CHOL 3mg; IRON 0.9mg; SODIUM 24mg; CALC 84mg

You hardly notice the small seeds when you pop a fresh raspberry, strawberry, or blueberry into your mouth. But when you want a velvety smooth texture for a soup or dessert sauce, you'll need to remove the seeds. Straining the berry mixture through a sieve separates the fruit juice and pulp from the seeds.

Be creative and consider serving this cool, fruity starter in wine or parfait glasses as an alternative to a traditional bowl. The presentation will take your recipe from simple to sensational!

Winter Plum Soup

When you are blending hot liquids, use caution because steam can increase the pressure inside the blender and blow off the lid. Don't fill the blender more than halfway, and blend in batches, if necessary. Let the mixture cool, uncovered, in the blender for a few minutes. Also, be sure to hold a potholder or towel over the lid when blending.

2 (16-ounce) cans plums in light syrup, undrained
2 cups dry red wine
1 tablespoon honey
½ teaspoon ground cinnamon
¼ teaspoon ground cloves
¼ cup Cointreau or other orange-flavored liqueur
½ teaspoon grated lemon rind
6 tablespoons vanilla low-fat yogurt
6 mint sprigs (optional)

1. Strain plums through a sieve into a bowl, reserving juice. Cut plums in half; discard pits. Combine plums, reserved juice, wine, honey, cinnamon, and cloves in a medium saucepan. Bring to a boil. Cover; reduce heat, and simmer 15 minutes. Place half of soup in a blender; process until smooth. Pour into a bowl. Repeat procedure with remaining soup. Stir in liqueur and rind. Ladle ¾ cup soup into each of 6 wine goblets. Top each serving with 1 tablespoon yogurt and 1 mint sprig, if desired. Yield: 6 servings.

CALORIES 133 (3% from fat); FAT 0.4g (sat 0.1g, mono 0.2g, poly 0.1g); PROTEIN 1.5g; CARB 32g; FIBER 1.5g; CHOL 1mg; IRON 1.7mg; SODIUM 47mg; CALC 49mg

This rosy purée of canned plums, wine, and Cointreau is equally good served warm, at room temperature, or chilled. It makes a wonderful first course or a refreshingly light dessert. Prepare up to one day ahead and chill in the refrigerator, allowing the flavors to meld before serving.

Vichyssoise

With a sweeter and more delicate flavor than onions, leeks add a subtle touch to recipes without overpowering the other flavors that are present. Before preparing leeks, clean them thoroughly to remove any soil that may be caught between the overlapping layers. Trim the roots and a portion of the green tops. Remove the outer layer. Make a lengthwise cut to the center of each leek, fold it open, and run the leek under cool running water.

1 tablespoon canola oil
3 cups diced leek (about 3 large)
3 cups diced peeled baking potato (about 1¼ pounds)
1 (14-ounce) can fat-free, less-sodium chicken broth
⅔ cup half-and-half
¼ teaspoon salt
⅛ teaspoon black pepper
1 tablespoon minced fresh chives

1. Heat oil in a large saucepan over medium-low heat. Add leek; cover and cook 10 minutes or until soft. Stir in potato and broth; bring to a boil. Cover, reduce heat, and simmer 15 minutes or until potato is tender. Place in a blender or food processor; process until smooth. Place in a large bowl; cool to room temperature. Stir in half-and-half, salt, and pepper. Cover and chill. Ladle soup into individual bowls. Sprinkle with chives. Yield: 5 servings (serving size: 1 cup).

CALORIES 173 (35% from fat); FAT 6.7g (sat 2.5g, mono 2.7g, poly 1.1g); PROTEIN 4.4g; CARB 25.2g; FIBER 2.1g; CHOL 12mg; IRON 1.4mg; SODIUM 372mg; CALC 70mg

Formally known as crème vichyssoise glacée, *this cold potato and leek soup was created in 1910 by Louis Diat, who was chef at the Ritz-Carlton Hotel in New York. The name, loosely translated, means "coming from Vichy" (a French city near Diat's childhood home). Though traditionally served cold, this version is also good warm.*

White Velvet Soup

This unusual vegetable—knobby, hairy, and brown—is known as celeriac or celery root. Trim the ends and peel away the rough exterior, and you'll find creamy, white flesh with a mild flavor. Pick small to medium-sized roots that are firm and relatively clean. To peel celeriac, cut off the top and bottom, squaring off the bottom so the celeriac will sit securely on the cutting board. Using a sharp knife, cut around the sides to remove the outer layer.

4 cups (¼-inch) diced peeled celeriac (celery root; about 1¼ pounds)

4 cups (¼-inch) diced peeled Yukon gold potato (about 1¼ pounds)

3 cups fat-free, less-sodium chicken broth

2 cups water

2 tablespoons fresh thyme leaves

4 large garlic cloves, chopped

⅓ cup white wine

¾ teaspoon salt

½ cup 2% reduced-fat milk

1 tablespoon extravirgin olive oil

3 tablespoons thinly sliced green onions

1. Combine first 6 ingredients in a large stockpot; bring to a boil. Partially cover, reduce heat, and simmer 30 minutes or until vegetables are tender. Place half of potato mixture in a blender; process until smooth. Repeat with remaining potato mixture. Return puréed potato mixture to pan; stir in wine and salt. Cook over medium heat 3 minutes or until thoroughly heated. Remove soup from heat, and stir in milk.

2. Ladle soup into individual bowls; drizzle oil over soup. Sprinkle with onions. Yield: 6 servings (serving size: 1⅓ cups soup, ½ teaspoon oil, and 1½ teaspoons onions).

CALORIES 161 (17% from fat); FAT 3.1g (sat 0.7g, mono 2g, poly 0.4g); PROTEIN 6.4g; CARB 28.5g; FIBER 4.4g; CHOL 2mg; IRON 2.1mg; SODIUM 625mg; CALC 97mg

Celeriac and Yukon gold potatoes are the base of this deceptively rich soup. A drizzle of extravirgin olive oil at the end is a traditional method for adding subtle flavor and richness to the soup.

Fresh Tomato Soup

Plum tomatoes, also called Roma or Italian tomatoes, are the best year-round supermarket tomato, so you don't have to wait until summer to make this recipe. Plum tomatoes are a deep red color, and they have a distinctive oval shape. With firmer flesh and fewer seeds than round tomatoes, they are considered the best cooking tomatoes due to their concentrated flavor and high acidity.

1 teaspoon olive oil
1 cup chopped onion
4 cups chopped plum tomato (about 2 pounds)
3 (14-ounce) cans fat-free, less-sodium chicken broth
2 garlic cloves, crushed
7 cups chopped seeded peeled plum tomato (about 3 pounds)
¼ teaspoon salt
¼ teaspoon black pepper
1 teaspoon grated lemon rind
1 teaspoon butter
3 tablespoons thinly sliced fresh basil

1. Heat oil in a large saucepan over medium-high heat. Add onion, and sauté 4 minutes or until tender. Add 4 cups tomato; cook 2 minutes. Reduce heat to low; stir in broth and garlic. Simmer, covered, 30 minutes.

2. Uncover and simmer 45 minutes or until reduced to about 6 cups. Drain broth mixture through a sieve into a large bowl; discard solids. Return broth to pan. Stir in 7 cups tomato, salt, and pepper; bring to a boil. Reduce heat; simmer, uncovered, 10 minutes.

3. Remove soup from heat. Stir in rind and butter. Ladle soup into individual serving bowls. Sprinkle with basil. Yield: 6 servings (serving size: about 1 cup).

CALORIES 100 (19% from fat); FAT 2.1g (sat 0.6g, mono 0.9g, poly 0.5g); PROTEIN 6.3g; CARB 17.1g; FIBER 4g; CHOL 2mg; IRON 1mg; SODIUM 690mg; CALC 44mg

Tomato soup is second to chicken noodle soup in popularity. Homemade tomato stock provides the base for this soup. Prepare the soup through step 2 up to a day ahead. Reheat over medium-low heat, and add the lemon rind, butter, and basil just before serving.

Shrimp and Spinach Soup

Mirin, a staple in Japanese cuisine, is a variety of low-alcohol rice wine similar to sake. Its slightly sweet taste is often used to enhance the flavor of a dish, especially fish and seafood. It should, however, be used in small amounts, as its flavor is quite strong.

½ cup water
½ cup matchstick-cut peeled fresh ginger
¼ cup mirin (sweet rice wine)
2 tablespoons low-sodium soy sauce
2 (14-ounce) cans vegetable broth
1 pound medium shrimp, peeled and deveined
2 cups bagged prewashed spinach (about 2 ounces)

1. Combine first 5 ingredients in a large saucepan, and bring to a boil. Cover, reduce heat, and simmer 10 minutes. Stir in shrimp, and cook over medium heat 2 minutes or until shrimp are almost done. Stir in spinach, and cook 1 minute, stirring occasionally. Yield: 6 servings (serving size: about ¾ cup).

CALORIES 120 (14% from fat); FAT 1.9g (sat 0.3g, mono 0.2g, poly 0.5g); PROTEIN 17.1g; CARB 6.5g; FIBER 0.3g; CHOL 115mg; IRON 2.2mg; SODIUM 861mg; CALC 52mg

Vibrant green spinach leaves float in a yellow-hued mixture of sweet rice wine and vegetable broth. You can prepare the seasoned broth up to one day in advance, omitting the shrimp and spinach. Shortly before serving, reheat the broth, and stir them in.

Chilled Corn Bisque with Basil, Avocado, and Crab

A perfect bisque has a slightly thick, creamy texture. While a blender or food processor can transform food from chunky to smooth in a few seconds, vegetable skins are hard to purée completely. To get a completely smooth bisque, strain soup through a sieve. If the mixture is thick, you may need to use the back of a spoon to press the puréed soup through the sieve. Discard the solids that remain.

3 cups fat-free, less-sodium chicken broth
3 tablespoons cornstarch
1 tablespoon butter
1 cup finely chopped onion
1 garlic clove, minced
4 cups fresh corn kernels (about 8 ears)
¾ teaspoon salt
¼ teaspoon ground red pepper
½ cup 2% reduced-fat milk
½ cup half-and-half
8 ounces lump crabmeat, shell pieces removed (about 1½ cups)
⅓ cup chopped peeled avocado
3 tablespoons chopped fresh basil

1. Combine broth and cornstarch, stirring with a whisk.
2. Melt butter in a large saucepan over medium-high heat. Add onion; sauté 3 minutes. Add garlic; sauté 30 seconds. Stir in broth mixture, corn, salt, and pepper; bring to a simmer. Cook 7 minutes, stirring frequently (do not boil). Place half of corn mixture in a blender, and process until smooth. Pour puréed corn mixture into a large bowl. Repeat procedure with remaining corn mixture. Strain puréed corn mixture through a sieve into a large bowl; discard solids. Stir in milk and half-and-half, and chill thoroughly.
3. Stir well and ladle ⅔ cup soup into each of 8 bowls; top each serving with 3 tablespoons crab, about 2 teaspoons avocado, and about 1 teaspoon basil. Yield: 8 servings.

CALORIES 159 (30% from fat); FAT 5.3g (sat 2.4g, mono 1.9g, poly 0.7g); PROTEIN 10.8g; CARB 18g; FIBER 2.3g; CHOL 34mg; IRON 0.6mg; SODIUM 536mg; CALC 64mg

The flavor will come through better if you take off the chill. Allow soup to stand at room temperature for about 30 minutes before serving. Chop the avocado and the basil just before serving so they don't begin to brown.

Roasted Squash Soup with Turkey Croquettes

Butternut squash has a firm texture, making it difficult to cut. The secret is to microwave it whole on HIGH 1 to 2 minutes. This step helps soften the winter squash for slicing. After microwaving, cut the squash in half lengthwise; remove and discard seeds.

Soup:

- 2 pounds butternut squash
- 1 tablespoon honey
- ¼ teaspoon kosher salt
- ¼ teaspoon freshly ground black pepper
- 1 teaspoon canola oil
- ¾ cup finely chopped onion
- ½ cup finely chopped carrot
- ¼ cup finely chopped celery
- 3 garlic cloves, minced
- 4 cups fat-free, less-sodium chicken broth
- 1 cup 2% reduced-fat milk
- ¼ teaspoon kosher salt

Dash of freshly ground black pepper

Croquettes:

- 2 cups finely chopped cooked turkey or chicken
- 1¾ cups panko (Japanese) breadcrumbs, divided
- 2 tablespoons 2% reduced-fat milk
- 1½ teaspoons chopped fresh sage
- ½ teaspoon salt

Dash of freshly ground black pepper

- 1 large egg, lightly beaten
- 1 large egg white
- 2½ tablespoons canola oil, divided

Sage leaves (optional)

1. Preheat oven to 400°.

2. To prepare soup, cut squash in half lengthwise. Discard seeds and membrane. Place squash, cut sides up, on a foil-lined baking sheet. Drizzle with honey; sprinkle with ¼ teaspoon salt and ¼ teaspoon pepper. Bake at 400° for 1 hour or until tender; cool. Scoop out squash with a spoon; discard skin.

3. Heat 1 teaspoon oil in a large saucepan over medium-high heat. Add onion, carrot, celery, and garlic; sauté 10 minutes or until tender. Remove ¾ cup vegetables; set aside. Add broth to pan; cook over medium heat 12 minutes. Stir in squash. Reduce heat; simmer 15 minutes. Place soup in a food processor; process until smooth. Add 1 cup milk, ¼ teaspoon salt, and dash of pepper; set aside.

4. To prepare croquettes, combine reserved vegetables, turkey, ¼ cup breadcrumbs, and next 6 ingredients. Cover and refrigerate 30 minutes or until firm. Shape into 12 (1-inch-thick) patties; press remaining 1½ cups breadcrumbs onto patties.

5. Heat 3¾ teaspoons oil in a nonstick skillet over medium heat. Add 6 patties to pan; cook 3 minutes on each side or until golden brown. Remove croquettes from pan; keep warm. Repeat procedure with remaining oil and patties.

6. Reheat soup over medium heat. Ladle soup into individual bowls; top with croquettes. Garnish with sage leaves, if desired. Yield: 4 servings (serving size: about 1½ cups soup and 3 croquettes).

CALORIES 602 (28% from fat); FAT 18g (sat 3.5g, mono 8.6g, poly 4.6g); PROTEIN 33g; CARB 77g; FIBER 11g; CHOL 100mg; IRON 4.5mg; SODIUM 1,375mg; CALC 282mg

smooth & creamy soups

Cream of Asparagus Soup

3 cups (½-inch) slices
   asparagus (about 1 pound)
2 cups fat-free, less-sodium
   chicken broth
¾ teaspoon chopped fresh
   thyme, divided
1 bay leaf
1 garlic clove, crushed
1 tablespoon all-purpose flour
2 cups 1% low-fat milk
Dash of ground nutmeg
2 teaspoons butter
¾ teaspoon salt
¼ teaspoon grated lemon rind

1. Combine asparagus, broth, ½ teaspoon thyme, bay leaf, and crushed garlic in a large saucepan over medium-high heat; bring to a boil. Cover, reduce heat, and simmer 10 minutes. Discard bay leaf. Place asparagus mixture in a blender; process until smooth.

2. Place flour in pan. Gradually add milk, stirring with a whisk until blended. Add puréed asparagus and ground nutmeg; stir to combine. Bring to a boil. Reduce heat, and simmer 5 minutes, stirring constantly. Remove from heat, and stir in remaining ¼ teaspoon thyme, butter, salt, and rind. Yield: 4 servings (serving size: 1¼ cups).

CALORIES 117 (27% from fat); FAT 3.5g (sat 2g, mono 0.8g, poly 0.2g); PROTEIN 8.9g; CARB 14g; FIBER 2.5g; CHOL 13mg; IRON 1.1mg; SODIUM 748mg; CALC 163mg

The key to a delicious cream of asparagus soup is the asparagus, of course. Asparagus has a mild flavor and a delicate texture, although it becomes tougher as it ages. During its peak season (February through June), pencil-thin spears are plentiful. To maintain freshness, wrap a moist paper towel around the stem ends, or stand upright in about 2 inches of cold water.

Garnish this soup with thin asparagus spears for a graceful presentation. Serve this springtime sensation with a shrimp salad and melba toast.

Savory Beet Soup

1 teaspoon olive oil
1 cup chopped onion
4 cups fat-free, less-sodium
    chicken broth
2 cups water
½ teaspoon salt
¼ teaspoon freshly ground
    black pepper
3 beets, peeled and halved
1 medium baking potato,
    peeled and halved crosswise
1 bay leaf
1 teaspoon lemon juice
8 teaspoons reduced-fat sour
    cream

1. Heat oil in a Dutch oven over medium-high heat. Add onion; sauté 2 minutes or until tender. Add broth and next 6 ingredients. Bring to a boil; reduce heat, and simmer, uncovered, 20 minutes or until beets and potato are tender. Discard bay leaf.

2. Place one-third of broth mixture in a blender or food processor; process until smooth. Place puréed mixture in a large bowl. Repeat procedure twice with remaining broth mixture. Return puréed mixture to pan. Warm soup over low heat 5 minutes or until thoroughly heated. Remove from heat, and stir in lemon juice.

3. Combine ½ cup soup and sour cream, stirring with a whisk. Ladle soup into individual bowls. Top each serving with 1 tablespoon sour cream mixture; swirl sour cream mixture using tip of a knife. Yield: 8 servings (serving size: about ¾ cup soup).

CALORIES 74 (16% from fat); FAT 1.3g (sat 0.5g, mono 0.4g, poly 0.1g); PROTEIN 3.3g; CARB 12.3g; FIBER 2.2g; CHOL 3mg; IRON 0.7mg; SODIUM 343mg; CALC 23mg

This firm, round root vegetable ranges in color from white to deep red, and it has a large leafy top. When cooked, it has a sweet, earthy flavor and a tender texture. Fresh beets are available year-round but are most abundant from March through July. Look for small to medium well-shaped beets with smooth skins. Very large beets may be tough. If leaves are attached, they should be crisp and bright green. When cut, beets stain everything they touch, including hands and cutting boards. One smart tip for handling beets is to wear disposable latex gloves. They're thin enough to allow dexterity while protecting hands from stains.

This rich, velvety soup is a mild version of borscht, a traditional soup made with beets, cabbage, and potatoes. We opted to omit the cabbage and to purée the soup to a smooth consistency. Ideal for autumn, this soup is ravishingly rich and comfortably creamy. For added creaminess and a lovely presentation, we swirled this vibrantly colored soup with sour cream.

Carrot-Parsnip Soup with Parsnip Chips

Parsnips are root vegetables with a sweet, nutty flavor. The long, tapering vegetable is shaped like a carrot and has beige-white skin. Parsnips can be refrigerated in a plastic bag up to a month; they are suitable for baking, boiling, sautéing, roasting, or steaming and are often boiled and mashed like potatoes or served in combination with potatoes. They are wonderful roasted; it brings out their sweetness.

2 tablespoons olive oil, divided
2½ cups chopped yellow onion
3 cups coarsely chopped parsnip (about 1 pound)
3 cups water
2½ cups coarsely chopped carrot (about 1 pound)
2 (14-ounce) cans fat-free, less-sodium chicken broth
¼ teaspoon salt
¼ teaspoon freshly ground black pepper
½ cup (⅛-inch-thick) slices parsnip
1 tablespoon chopped fresh chives

1. Heat 1 teaspoon oil in a Dutch oven over medium heat. Add onion; cook 10 minutes or until tender, stirring occasionally. Add chopped parsnip, water, carrot, and broth; bring to a boil. Reduce heat, and simmer 50 minutes or until vegetables are tender. Remove from heat; let stand 5 minutes.

2. Place half of carrot mixture in a blender; process until smooth. Pour puréed carrot mixture into a large bowl. Repeat procedure with remaining carrot mixture. Stir in salt and pepper.

3. Heat remaining 5 teaspoons oil in a small saucepan over medium-high heat. Add parsnip slices; cook 5 minutes or until lightly browned, turning occasionally. Drain on paper towels. Ladle soup into individual bowls. Sprinkle parsnip chips and chives over soup. Serve immediately. Yield: 6 servings (serving size: 1⅓ cups soup, about 2 teaspoons parsnip chips, and ½ teaspoon chives).

CALORIES 159 (28% from fat); FAT 4.9g (sat 0.7g, mono 3.4g, poly 0.6g); PROTEIN 3.7g; CARB 26.4g; FIBER 6.4g; CHOL 0mg; IRON 0.8mg; SODIUM 388mg; CALC 61mg

Winter root vegetables lend their complementary, slightly sweet flavors to this hearty soup. Stir in more water or broth if you prefer a thinner consistency.

Canadian Cheese Soup with Pumpernickel Croutons

When chopping the onion, carrot, and celery in a food processor, pulse until the vegetables are roughly the size of small peas. For the best results, cut the vegetables into pieces of similar size and length before placing them in the processor.

3 (1-ounce) slices pumpernickel bread, cut into ½-inch cubes
1 onion, peeled and quartered
1 carrot, peeled and quartered
1 celery stalk, quartered
1 teaspoon butter
¾ cup all-purpose flour
2 (14-ounce) cans fat-free, less-sodium chicken broth
3 cups 2% reduced-fat milk
½ teaspoon salt
½ teaspoon paprika
½ teaspoon freshly ground black pepper
1½ cups (6 ounces) reduced-fat shredded sharp Cheddar cheese

1. Preheat oven to 375°.

2. Place bread cubes on a jelly-roll pan, and bake at 375° for 15 minutes or until toasted.

3. Combine onion, carrot, and celery in a food processor, and pulse until chopped. Melt butter in a Dutch oven over medium-high heat. Add vegetables; sauté 5 minutes or until tender.

4. Lightly spoon flour into dry measuring cups; level with a knife. Gradually add 1 can broth to flour in a medium bowl; stir well with a whisk. Add flour mixture to pan. Stir in remaining 1 can broth; bring to a boil. Reduce heat to medium; cook 10 minutes or until thick. Stir in milk, salt, paprika, and pepper; cook 10 minutes. Remove from heat. Add cheese; stir until cheese melts. Ladle soup into individual bowls, and top with croutons. Yield: 8 servings (serving size: 1 cup soup and ¼ cup croutons).

CALORIES 203 (30% from fat); FAT 6.8g (sat 3.8g, mono 1.9g, poly 0.4g); PROTEIN 13.2g; CARB 21.9g; FIBER 1.8g; CHOL 23mg; IRON 1.1mg; SODIUM 671mg; CALC 318mg

Pair this savory soup with a green salad and a bowl of chopped fruit for a simple, satisfying meal.

Pumpkin-Pear Soup with Maple Cream

Fresh pumpkins are available in the fall and winter, and most will keep for a month or longer if stored in a cool, dry place. Once cut, pumpkins should be wrapped tightly in plastic, refrigerated, and used within three or four days. You can substitute other winter squash, such as butternut or kabocha, if pumpkin is not available.

1 tablespoon butter
1 cup chopped onion
1 tablespoon brown sugar
½ teaspoon ground cumin
5 cups cubed peeled pumpkin
   or other winter squash
   (about 2½ pounds)
3 cups fat-free, less-sodium
   chicken broth
½ teaspoon salt
2 cups coarsely chopped
   peeled ripe Bartlett pear
   (about 2)
¼ cup reduced-fat sour cream
2 tablespoons maple syrup
Thyme sprigs (optional)

1. Melt butter in a Dutch oven over medium heat. Add onion, brown sugar, and cumin; cook 5 minutes or until onions are tender, stirring occasionally.
2. Add pumpkin, broth, and salt, and bring to a boil over medium-high heat. Add pear; cover, reduce heat, and simmer 5 minutes or until pumpkin is tender.
3. Remove from heat. Cool slightly. Place half of pumpkin mixture in a blender; process until smooth. Pour into a large bowl. Repeat procedure with remaining pumpkin mixture. Return puréed mixture to pan; keep warm.
4. Combine sour cream and maple syrup. Ladle soup into individual bowls, and drizzle maple cream over each serving. Garnish soup with thyme sprigs, if desired. Yield: 8 servings (serving size: 1 cup soup and about 2 teaspoons maple cream).

CALORIES 120 (21% from fat); FAT 2.8g (sat 1.4g, mono 0.6g, poly 0.1g); PROTEIN 3.4g; CARB 23.4g; FIBER 2g; CHOL 8mg; IRON 1.3mg; SODIUM 398mg; CALC 58mg

Pumpkin deserves to be more than a once-a-year pie filling. Here, it stars with sweet, ripe pears in a silky and succulent first course for a late fall or winter evening. Serve the soup with poppy seed breadsticks made from refrigerated dough.

Curry-Ginger-Butternut Squash Soup

Named after a seaside town in Thailand, Sriracha is a hot chile sauce that includes red Thai chiles, sugar, vinegar, salt, and garlic. The flavor is a combination of sweet and sour and hot and spicy. The most common brand, Huy Fong, comes in a clear plastic squeeze bottle with a rooster on the label and a bright green cap. It's enjoyed as a table condiment in Thai and Vietnamese restaurants, but it's also great with non-Asian dishes, such as this butternut squash soup. Try it in place of ketchup on almost anything—french fries, omelets or scrambled eggs, pizza, hot dogs, and hamburgers.

2 teaspoons canola oil
3 tablespoons finely chopped peeled fresh ginger
3 garlic cloves, minced
2 teaspoons curry powder
1 cup mirin (sweet rice wine)
6 cups (½-inch) cubed peeled butternut squash (about 2½ pounds)
6 cups fat-free, less-sodium chicken broth
2½ cups (½-inch) cubed peeled celeriac (celery root; 1 to 1½ pounds)
2 teaspoons thawed orange juice concentrate
1 teaspoon Sriracha (hot chile sauce, such as Huy Fong)
½ teaspoon salt
½ cup plain low-fat yogurt
2 teaspoons chopped fresh flat-leaf parsley

1. Heat oil in a Dutch oven over medium-high heat. Add ginger and garlic; sauté 1½ minutes. Add curry; cook 15 seconds, stirring constantly. Add mirin; cook until liquid is reduced to ½ cup (about 4 minutes). Add squash, broth, and celeriac; bring to a boil. Reduce heat; simmer 15 minutes or until tender.

2. Place one-fourth of squash mixture in a blender; process until smooth. Strain puréed squash mixture through a sieve into a large bowl; discard solids. Repeat procedure in 3 more batches with remaining squash mixture. Stir in orange juice concentrate, Sriracha, and salt. Ladle soup into individual bowls. Dollop 1 tablespoon yogurt over each serving, and sprinkle with parsley. Yield: 8 servings (serving size: about 1 cup).

CALORIES 206 (8% from fat); FAT 1.8g (sat 0.3g, mono 0.8g, poly 0.5g); PROTEIN 5.8g; CARB 38.3g; FIBER 4.7g; CHOL 1mg; IRON 1.8mg; SODIUM 653mg; CALC 140mg

If it's fall, then it's time for butternut squash. Straining this spicy-sweet, golden-hued soup gives the final product a velvety appearance and texture. Swirl in a dollop of yogurt, and you've got a soup that's as pretty as the colorful leaves outside your kitchen window.

Golden Summer Soup

This recipe uses four fresh herbs: chervil, chives, basil, and parsley. Their fragrant leaves are used to garnish the colorful soup. When storing the herbs, douse the leaves with cool water, and wrap the stems in a damp paper towel. Place the towel-wrapped herbs in a zip-top plastic bag, and refrigerate up to a week.

Cooking spray
2 garlic cloves, minced
8 cups chopped yellow tomato (about 3½ pounds)
3 cups chopped Vidalia or other sweet onion
2 cups fresh corn kernels
1 cup chopped yellow bell pepper
1 teaspoon fine sea salt
1 teaspoon grated lemon rind
½ teaspoon freshly ground black pepper
½ teaspoon hot sauce
1 tablespoon coarsely chopped fresh chervil
1 tablespoon coarsely chopped fresh chives
1 tablespoon coarsely chopped fresh basil
1 tablespoon coarsely chopped fresh flat-leaf parsley
1 cup halved cherry or grape tomatoes

1. Heat a small Dutch oven over medium-high heat. Coat pan with cooking spray. Add garlic; sauté 15 seconds. Add yellow tomato, onion, corn, and bell pepper; bring to a boil. Reduce heat, and simmer 15 minutes or until onion is tender, stirring occasionally. Place half of tomato mixture in a blender; process until smooth. Press puréed tomato mixture through a large sieve into a large bowl, reserving liquid; discard solids. Repeat procedure with remaining tomato mixture. Stir in salt, lemon rind, black pepper, and hot sauce.

2. Combine chervil, chives, basil, and parsley, tossing gently. Ladle 1¼ cups soup into each of 4 bowls; top each with ¼ cup cherry tomatoes and 1 tablespoon herb mixture. Yield: 4 servings.

CALORIES 209 (12% from fat); FAT 2.7g (sat 0.4g, mono 0.5g, poly 1.2g); PROTEIN 9.2g; CARB 46.8g; FIBER 11.8g; CHOL 0mg; IRON 3.2mg; SODIUM 636mg; CALC 82mg

This colorful soup has a velvety texture. The garnish of fresh-from-the-garden herbs and tomatoes adds a bright burst of flavor and an appealing textural contrast.

Creamy Tomato-Balsamic Soup

1 cup less-sodium beef broth, divided
1 tablespoon brown sugar
3 tablespoons balsamic vinegar
1 tablespoon low-sodium soy sauce
1 cup coarsely chopped onion
5 garlic cloves
2 (28-ounce) cans whole tomatoes, drained
Cooking spray
¾ cup half-and-half
Cracked black pepper (optional)

1. Preheat oven to 500°.
2. Combine ½ cup broth, sugar, vinegar, and soy sauce in a small bowl. Place chopped onion, garlic, and tomatoes in a 13 x 9–inch baking pan coated with cooking spray. Pour broth mixture over tomato mixture. Bake at 500° for 50 minutes or until vegetables are lightly browned.
3. Place tomato mixture in a blender. Add remaining ½ cup broth and half-and-half, and process until smooth. Strain mixture through a sieve into a bowl; discard solids. Ladle soup into individual bowls. Garnish with cracked black pepper, if desired. Yield: 4 servings (serving size: about ½ cup).

CALORIES 120 (35% from fat); FAT 4.7g (sat 3g, mono 1.5g, poly 0.1g); PROTEIN 3.8g; CARB 14.9g; FIBER 1.7g; CHOL 23mg; IRON 1.7mg; SODIUM 452mg; CALC 120mg

Cooking the vegetables at the high temperature of 500° caramelizes their natural sugars and deepens their flavor; the liquid poured over them ensures they won't burn. Use a baking or roasting pan when roasting vegetables.

With summer's heat gone and winter's chill yet to come, the cool days of fall offer a welcomed opportunity for alfresco dining in your own backyard or on a roadside picnic during a leaf-viewing drive. Rosy tomato soup reflects the changing colors of the season and offers a rich taste befitting this time of year.

quick &
easy soups

Springtime Risotto Soup

Arborio rice is an Italian-grown rice that's shorter, plumper, and higher in starch content than long-grain rice. Sautéing rice with onion in hot oil or butter infuses the rice with flavor. Gradually stirring in the broth with a wooden spoon gives the starch in the rice time to dissolve and form a creamy sauce that complements the chewy rice.

1 tablespoon olive oil
2 cups chopped onion
2 teaspoons grated lemon rind
¾ cup Arborio rice or other short-grain rice
3 (14-ounce) cans fat-free, less-sodium chicken broth
2 cups (1-inch) slices asparagus (about 1 pound)
2 cups coarsely chopped spinach
¼ teaspoon ground nutmeg
½ cup (2 ounces) grated fresh Parmesan cheese

1. Heat oil in a large saucepan over medium-high heat. Add onion; sauté 2 minutes. Add rind; sauté 2 minutes. Add rice; sauté 3 minutes.
2. Stir in chicken broth; bring to a boil. Cover, reduce heat, and simmer 10 minutes. Stir in asparagus, spinach, and nutmeg; cook, uncovered, 2 minutes or until asparagus is crisp-tender. Ladle soup into individual bowls, and top each serving with Parmesan cheese. Serve immediately. Yield: 4 servings (serving size: 1¾ cups soup and 2 tablespoons cheese).

CALORIES 320 (21% from fat); FAT 7.5g (sat 2.9g, mono 3.6g, poly 0.5g); PROTEIN 14.9g; CARB 46.2g; FIBER 4.1g; CHOL 10mg; IRON 1.6mg; SODIUM 815mg; CALC 234mg

If you love the flavor and creamy texture of traditional risotto but don't have the time or patience needed to gradually stir the hot broth into the rice, this soup is a must-try for you.

Chickpea Stew Scented with Lemon and Cumin

Traditional polenta is made by cooking coarse cornmeal with liquid to form a soft mush. Soft polenta is delicious served warm with butter or as an alternative to rice, pasta, or mashed potatoes. Soft polenta can be cooled until firm and then sliced for grilling, frying, or sautéing. Dry instant polenta is available in most supermarkets; it cooks in about 5 minutes, while regular polenta takes about 30 minutes to prepare.

4 cups water
1 cup instant dry polenta
1 tablespoon butter
1 tablespoon olive oil
1 cup chopped onion
1½ teaspoons bottled minced garlic
¼ cup lemon juice
1 teaspoon ground cumin
¼ teaspoon black pepper
2 (15-ounce) cans chickpeas (garbanzo beans), rinsed and drained
2 (14.5-ounce) cans diced tomatoes, undrained
½ cup chopped green onions
¾ cup reduced-fat sour cream

1. Bring water to a boil in a medium saucepan. Gradually add polenta, stirring constantly with a whisk. Reduce heat, and simmer 3 minutes, stirring frequently. Remove from heat; stir in butter. Cover and set aside.

2. While polenta cooks, heat oil in a large nonstick skillet over medium-high heat. Add onion and garlic; sauté 3 minutes. Add lemon juice, cumin, pepper, chickpeas, and tomatoes; bring to a boil. Reduce heat; simmer 6 minutes. Stir in green onions. Spoon polenta into individual bowls. Ladle stew over polenta. Top with sour cream. Yield: 6 servings (serving size: 1⅓ cups stew, ⅔ cup polenta, and 2 tablespoons sour cream).

CALORIES 400 (22% from fat); FAT 9.6g (sat 4g, mono 2.6g, poly 1g); PROTEIN 12.9g; CARB 68g; FIBER 9.8g; CHOL 21mg; IRON 2.8mg; SODIUM 838mg; CALC 180mg

From start to finish, this hearty, one-dish meatless meal can be on the table in less than 20 minutes. The chickpeas provide plenty of protein, and the polenta gives the dish a creamy base.

Mexican Black-Bean Chili

1 cup diced onion
1 cup diced green bell pepper
1 pound ground chuck
1 tablespoon chili powder
1½ teaspoons ground cumin
¾ teaspoon dried oregano
½ teaspoon salt
⅛ teaspoon black pepper
2 (15-ounce) cans black beans, rinsed and drained
2 (14.5-ounce) cans no salt–added diced tomatoes, undrained
1 (14-ounce) can fat-free, less-sodium beef broth
3 garlic cloves, crushed
6 tablespoons fat-free sour cream
Cilantro sprigs (optional)

1. Cook first 3 ingredients in a large nonstick skillet over medium-high heat until browned, stirring to crumble. Drain well; return meat mixture to pan. Add chili powder and next 8 ingredients; bring to a boil. Reduce heat; simmer 20 minutes or until slightly thick, stirring occasionally.
2. Ladle chili into individual bowls; top with sour cream. Garnish with cilantro sprigs, if desired. Yield: 6 servings (serving size: 1½ cups chili and 1 tablespoon sour cream).

CALORIES 236 (15% from fat); FAT 4g (sat 1.5g, mono 1.4g, poly 0.5g); PROTEIN 23.6g; CARB 33.6g; FIBER 10.5g; CHOL 41mg; IRON 4.3mg; SODIUM 884mg; CALC 112mg

Many shortcut chili recipes start with a packaged seasoning mix, which can be high in sodium. Instead of using packaged mixes, keep a variety of dried herbs and spices on hand to create your own flavor blends. But remember that dried herbs and spices lose their flavors over time. Use the smell test: If the dried herb or spice doesn't emit an aroma when the jar is opened, it's time to replace it. Store dried herbs and ground spices in a cool, dark place, as heat and sunlight hasten flavor loss.

Chili is one big melting pot of worldly influences. Here, we've highlighted south-of-the-border spices and the traditional use of black beans. Fast and flavorful, this chili fits the bill.

Sausage, Kale, and Bean Soup

4 ounces Cajun smoked sausage, chopped (such as Conecuh)
3 cups fat-free, less-sodium chicken broth
1 (14.5-ounce) can no salt–added diced tomatoes, undrained
6 cups coarsely chopped kale (about 8 ounces)
1 (16-ounce) can navy beans, rinsed and drained

1. Heat a large saucepan over medium-high heat. Add sausage; cook 2 minutes, stirring occasionally. Add broth and tomatoes; bring to a boil over high heat. Stir in kale. Reduce heat; simmer 4 minutes or until kale is tender. Stir in beans; cook 1 minute or until thoroughly heated. Yield: 4 servings (serving size: 1¾ cups).

CALORIES 280 (29% from fat); FAT 9g (sat 3.2g, mono 3.8g, poly 1.4g); PROTEIN 17g; CARB 33.6g; FIBER 2.8g; CHOL 20mg; IRON 3.4mg; SODIUM 924mg; CALC 153mg

Sausage is traditionally high in fat; however, a little goes a long way to add full flavor to dishes. All sausages are a mixture of chopped or ground meat and fat mixed with salt and other seasonings. Spicy sausage in particular can pack the most punch in small amounts. Many varieties exist, but the most well-known in the U.S. is Cajun-style, which is the spiciest of all.

Cajun sausage fires up a simple five-ingredient soup with smoky spice. Add some crusty bread, and you've got a meal on the table in no time.

Tuscan Chicken Stew

"White bean" is a generic term used for a variety of ivory-white beans. We call for cannellini beans (sometimes referred to as white kidney beans) in this chicken stew, but any other white bean (such as Great Northern beans or navy beans) may be substituted.

½ teaspoon dried rosemary, crushed
½ teaspoon salt
¼ teaspoon black pepper
1 pound skinless, boneless chicken breast, cut into 1-inch pieces
2 teaspoons olive oil
2 teaspoons bottled minced garlic
½ cup fat-free, less-sodium chicken broth
1 (16-ounce) can cannellini beans or other white beans, rinsed and drained
1 (7-ounce) bottle roasted red bell peppers, drained and cut into ½-inch pieces
3½ cups torn spinach

1. Combine first 4 ingredients, and toss well. Heat olive oil in a large nonstick skillet over medium-high heat. Add chicken mixture, and sauté 3 minutes. Add garlic, and sauté 1 minute. Add broth, beans, and bell peppers; bring to a boil. Reduce heat, and simmer 10 minutes or until chicken is done. Stir in spinach, and simmer 1 minute. Yield: 4 servings (serving size: 1 cup).

CALORIES 290 (18% from fat); FAT 5.9g (sat 0.9g, mono 2.4g, poly 1.4g); PROTEIN 34.8g; CARB 25.1g; FIBER 5.1g; CHOL 66mg; IRON 4.5mg; SODIUM 612mg; CALC 110mg

Make your home a Tuscan villa tonight with this Italian-inspired stew. Bake biscuits from a low-fat buttermilk baking mix while the stew simmers.

Turkey-Pasta Soup

You'll find napa cabbage in various shapes, from round to more elongated. It's similar in appearance to romaine lettuce and is thin and delicate with a mild flavor.

1 tablespoon olive oil
½ cup chopped carrot
¼ cup chopped celery
¼ cup minced onion
1 garlic clove, minced
2 cups water
⅓ cup chopped 33%-less-sodium ham (about 2 ounces)
¼ teaspoon freshly ground black pepper
4 (14-ounce) cans fat-free, less-sodium chicken broth
1 cup uncooked ditali (short tube-shaped macaroni)
3 cups chopped cooked turkey
3 cups thinly sliced napa (Chinese) cabbage

1. Heat oil in a large Dutch oven over medium-high heat. Add carrot, celery, onion, and garlic; sauté 3 minutes or until tender. Add water, ham, pepper, and broth; bring to a boil. Add pasta; cook 8 minutes or until pasta is done. Stir in turkey and cabbage, and cook 2 minutes or until cabbage wilts. Yield: 8 servings (serving size: 1½ cups).

CALORIES 194 (23% from fat); FAT 4.9g (sat 1.3g, mono 2g, poly 1g); PROTEIN 21.8g; CARB 14.2g; FIBER 1.2g; CHOL 44mg; IRON 1.6mg; SODIUM 483mg; CALC 45mg

Holiday leftovers star in this quick and simple recipe that is excellent for a casual meal. To ensure that the pasta cooks properly, make sure the soup is boiling when you add the ditali and that it comes back to a boil for the remaining cook time.

Turkey Soup Provençal

1 pound ground turkey breast
½ teaspoon dried herbes de Provence, crushed
1 (15-ounce) can cannellini beans or other white beans, rinsed and drained
1 (14.5-ounce) can diced tomatoes with garlic and onion, undrained
1 (14-ounce) can fat-free, less-sodium chicken broth
4 cups chopped fresh spinach

1. Cook turkey in a large saucepan over medium-high heat until browned, stirring to crumble.

2. Add herbes de Provence, beans, tomatoes, and broth to pan; bring to a boil. Reduce heat; simmer 5 minutes. Stir in spinach, and simmer 5 minutes. Yield: 4 servings (serving size: 1¼ cups).

CALORIES 294 (12% from fat); FAT 3.8g (sat 1.5g, mono 0.8g, poly 0.4g); PROTEIN 40g; CARB 25.4g; FIBER 5.4g; CHOL 75mg; IRON 6.1mg; SODIUM 890mg; CALC 206mg

Herbes de Provence is a mixture of dried herbs native to the Provence region of southern France. It traditionally contains rosemary, basil, bay leaves, and thyme. Other herbs, including savory, lavender, fennel seeds, and dried sage, are sometimes added. The proportion of the herbs in the mixture varies depending on the manufacturer. Herbes de Provence is used to flavor grilled meat or fish and side dishes such as potatoes, rice, or pasta.

Serve this quick-to-prepare soup with crusty French bread for a weeknight meal. Heat up your leftovers the next day for lunch.

North Woods Bean Soup

Hearty soups call for hearty ingredients, and chunky pieces of carrot add to the texture of this comforting dish. Baby carrots save prep time because they're already peeled, and cutting them in half lengthwise shortens the cook time.

Cooking spray
1 cup baby carrots, halved
1 cup chopped onion
2 garlic cloves, minced
7 ounces turkey kielbasa, halved lengthwise and cut into ½-inch pieces
4 cups fat-free, less-sodium chicken broth
½ teaspoon dried Italian seasoning
½ teaspoon black pepper
2 (15.8-ounce) cans Great Northern beans, rinsed and drained
1 (6-ounce) bag fresh baby spinach

1. Heat a large saucepan over medium-high heat. Coat pan with cooking spray. Add carrots, onion, garlic, and kielbasa; sauté 3 minutes. Reduce heat to medium; cook 5 minutes. Add broth, Italian seasoning, pepper, and beans. Bring to a boil; reduce heat, and simmer 5 minutes.
2. Place 2 cups soup in a food processor or blender, and process until smooth. Return puréed mixture to pan. Simmer 5 minutes. Remove soup from heat. Add spinach, stirring until spinach wilts. Yield: 5 servings (serving size: about 1½ cups).

CALORIES 227 (15% from fat); FAT 3.9g (sat 1.2g, mono 1.3g, poly 1.2g); PROTEIN 18.1g; CARB 30.8g; FIBER 6.7g; CHOL 26mg; IRON 3.5mg; SODIUM 750mg; CALC 112mg

You may not be a North Woods lumberjack, but you may enjoy eating like one. Puréeing some of the soup lends body to the dish. Stir in the fresh spinach after the soup is removed from the heat so it won't overcook and lose its bright color.

hearty soups & stews

Beef Burgundy Stew

Burgundy (*Bourgogne* in French) is the name given to certain dry wines produced in the Burgundy region of eastern France. France has rigid wine laws with regard to all aspects of wine making that help control the methods and quality of wine production. These laws help ensure that the wines labeled as Burgundy are authentic. Since the meat is braised in the wine for this classic dish, choose quality Burgundy for the biggest impact of flavor. Domestic dry red wine such as a shiraz may be substituted for the Burgundy.

2 teaspoons canola oil
Cooking spray
1½ pounds lean boneless round steak (½ inch thick), trimmed and cut into 1-inch cubes
2 large garlic cloves, minced
3 cups Burgundy or other dry red wine
¼ cup tomato paste
½ teaspoon dried thyme
2 bay leaves
½ cup water
2 (14-ounce) cans beef broth
10 small red potatoes, quartered (about 1½ pounds)
6 medium carrots, cut into 1-inch pieces (about 1 pound)
2 small onions, quartered (about ½ pound)
1 (8-ounce) package mushrooms, halved
3 tablespoons water
3 tablespoons cornstarch
½ teaspoon salt
¼ teaspoon black pepper
Chopped fresh parsley (optional)

1. Heat oil in a large Dutch oven coated with cooking spray over medium-high heat. Add steak, and cook 8 minutes on all sides or until browned. Add garlic; sauté 1 minute. Add wine, tomato paste, thyme, and bay leaves; bring mixture to a boil. Cover, reduce heat, and simmer 50 minutes.

2. Add ½ cup water and next 4 ingredients; bring to a boil. Cover, reduce heat, and simmer 40 minutes.

3. Stir in mushrooms; cover and cook 50 minutes or until steak is tender. Discard bay leaves.

4. Combine 3 tablespoons water and cornstarch in a small bowl; add to pan. Cook 2 minutes or until thickened, stirring constantly. Stir in salt and pepper. Ladle stew into individual bowls; sprinkle with parsley, if desired. Yield: 8 servings (serving size: about 1½ cups).

CALORIES 254 (15% from fat); FAT 4.2g (sat 1.1g, mono 1.7g, poly 0.6g); PROTEIN 23.9g; CARB 29.8g; FIBER 4g; CHOL 48mg; IRON 3.3mg; SODIUM 405mg; CALC 39mg

Perhaps the heartiest of all stews, the classic French boeuf bourguignon is streamlined here for calories and cooking techniques. But when it comes to flavor, this version is just as robust as the original. We added potatoes and carrots to make it a one-dish meal.

Savannah-Style Crab Soup

Flour plays two important roles in this recipe: It adds flavor and thickens the soup. When browning flour, stir the flour constantly with a whisk over medium heat. Watch the flour carefully so that it doesn't scorch and become bitter.

½ cup all-purpose flour
1 tablespoon butter
Cooking spray
2 cups chopped carrot
1 cup chopped celery
1 cup chopped onion
¼ cup chopped red bell pepper
¼ cup chopped green bell pepper
1 garlic clove, minced
1 tablespoon Old Bay seasoning
¼ teaspoon salt
¼ teaspoon black pepper
¼ teaspoon dried thyme
1 bay leaf
4 cups clam juice
1½ cups whole milk
½ cup half-and-half
1 pound lump crabmeat, shell pieces removed
⅓ cup dry sherry

1. Lightly spoon flour into a dry measuring cup; level with a knife. Place flour in a 9-inch cast-iron skillet; cook flour over medium heat 15 minutes or until brown, stirring constantly with a whisk. Remove from heat.
2. Melt butter in a Dutch oven coated with cooking spray over medium-high heat. Add carrot and next 5 ingredients; sauté 5 minutes or until vegetables are tender. Add Old Bay seasoning, salt, black pepper, dried thyme, and bay leaf; cook 1 minute. Sprinkle browned flour over vegetable mixture, and cook 1 minute, stirring frequently. Stir in clam juice; bring to a boil. Reduce heat, and simmer 10 minutes or until slightly thick, stirring frequently.
3. Stir in milk and half-and-half; cook 4 minutes. Stir in crabmeat and sherry; cook 5 minutes or until soup is thoroughly heated. Discard bay leaf. Yield: 9 servings (serving size: 1 cup).

CALORIES 151 (30% from fat); FAT 5g (sat 2.6g, mono 1.4g, poly 0.4g); PROTEIN 13g; CARB 13.3g; FIBER 1.8g; CHOL 46mg; IRON 2.2mg; SODIUM 835mg; CALC 112mg

Savannah-Style Crab Soup is reminiscent of she-crab soup—a Low Country (eastern South Carolina and Georgia) culinary hallmark. Popular in the South, it's traditionally flavored with sherry and made from the crabmeat and roe (the eggs) of fresh blue crabs. She-crab soup is a seasonal specialty because fresh crab roe is only produced in the spring. Our recipe simulates she-crab soup but omits the roe, as most restaurants do today, to ensure that a steady crop of crabs remains.

Braised Lamb Stew with Ginger

1 pound lamb stew meat
2 tablespoons cornstarch
1 tablespoon low-sodium soy
   sauce
1 tablespoon dry sherry
¼ teaspoon freshly ground
   black pepper
½ cup boiling water
6 dried shiitake mushrooms
1 tablespoon canola oil
2 tablespoons minced peeled
   fresh ginger
3 garlic cloves, minced
3 cups fat-free, less-sodium
   chicken broth
1⅓ cups sliced carrot
2 tablespoons oyster sauce
¼ cup chopped fresh cilantro
4 cups hot cooked rice
   noodles
Fresh cilantro leaves (optional)

1. Combine first 5 ingredients in a bowl.
2. Combine ½ cup boiling water and dried mushrooms in a bowl. Let stand 15 minutes; drain, reserving soaking liquid. Discard stems; thinly slice caps.
3. Heat oil in a large nonstick skillet over medium-high heat. Add ginger and garlic; sauté 30 seconds. Add lamb mixture; sauté 4 minutes. Stir in broth; bring to a boil. Cover and reduce heat; simmer 40 minutes. Uncover; bring to a boil. Add carrot, mushrooms, and reserved liquid. Cook 5 minutes or until slightly thickened. Add oyster sauce and chopped cilantro. Ladle stew into individual bowls; serve with rice noodles. Garnish with fresh cilantro, if desired. Yield: 4 servings (serving size: 1 cup stew and 1 cup noodles).

CALORIES 451 (20% from fat); FAT 10g (sat 2g, mono 5g, poly 2g); PROTEIN 28g; CARB 59g; FIBER 4g; CHOL 74mg; IRON 3mg; SODIUM 650mg; CALC 37mg

Shiitake mushrooms can be purchased either fresh or dried. When purchasing fresh mushrooms, the caps should be plump and dry. Dried shiitakes are often preferred to fresh because the drying process brings out their unique flavors. Soaking in boiling water rehydrates them. The soaking liquid makes a flavorful mushroom broth.

We've replaced the traditional rice with rice noodles to soak up the savory broth.

Spicy Sausage, Barley, and Mushroom Stew

Barley, a diet staple since the Stone Age, is a good source of fiber and potassium and is used frequently in cereals, breads, and soups. Two varieties of barley are most often found at grocery stores. The most nutritious form is whole-grain (hulled) barley, which has only the outer husk removed. It's most commonly used to make a thick, oat-meal-like cereal. Pearl barley is steamed and polished and works well in soups and stews. Quick-cooking barley, which takes only 20 minutes to prepare, is the most popular form of pearl barley.

2 teaspoons olive oil
2 cups thinly sliced onion
8 ounces spicy Italian turkey sausage
1 cup chopped celery
1 cup sliced carrot
2 garlic cloves, minced
1 bay leaf
5 cups thinly sliced shiitake mushroom caps
1½ cups chopped portobello mushrooms
½ cup uncooked pearl barley
3 (14-ounce) cans fat-free, less-sodium chicken broth
2 tablespoons brandy
1 teaspoon salt
¼ teaspoon freshly ground black pepper
6 tablespoons chopped fresh parsley

1. Heat oil in a large Dutch oven over medium heat. Add onion; cook 5 minutes or until tender. Remove casings from sausage. Add sausage to pan; cook 8 minutes or until sausage is browned, stirring to crumble. Add celery, carrot, garlic, and bay leaf; cook 10 minutes or until onion is golden brown, stirring frequently.

2. Stir in mushrooms, and cook 10 minutes or until liquid almost evaporates. Stir in barley, broth, brandy, salt, and pepper. Bring mixture to a boil; cover, reduce heat, and simmer 1 hour or until barley is tender. Discard bay leaf. Ladle soup into individual bowls. Sprinkle with parsley. Yield: 6 servings (serving size: about 1 cup stew and 1 tablespoon parsley).

CALORIES 213 (30% from fat); FAT 7.2g (sat 2g, mono 2.5g, poly 1.8g); PROTEIN 13.3g; CARB 23.4g; FIBER 4.7g; CHOL 27mg; IRON 2.4mg; SODIUM 481mg; CALC 54mg

While the sausage adds spice to this stew, it's the robust flavor of the mushrooms and the chewy texture of the barley that make it so filling.

Black Bean and Chorizo Chili

Chocolate can be found throughout Mexican cuisine in desserts, of course, but also in savory dishes. In this recipe, a small amount of semisweet chocolate adds to the chili's richness without adding sweetness.

Cooking spray
2 canned chipotle chiles in adobo sauce, drained and finely chopped
1¾ cups chopped onion
1½ cups chopped green bell pepper
1½ cups chopped red bell pepper
5 garlic cloves, minced
3 links Spanish chorizo sausage, diced (about 6½ ounces)
1½ tablespoons chili powder
1 tablespoon ground cumin
1½ teaspoons dried oregano
1 tablespoon fresh lime juice
⅛ teaspoon ground cinnamon
3 (15-ounce) cans black beans, rinsed and drained
3 (14-ounce) cans whole peeled tomatoes, undrained and chopped
1 (8½-ounce) can no salt–added whole-kernel corn, drained
1½ ounces semisweet chocolate, chopped
¾ teaspoon salt
½ teaspoon black pepper

1. Heat a large Dutch oven over medium-high heat. Coat pan with cooking spray. Add chiles, onion, bell peppers, garlic, and chorizo, and sauté 5 minutes or until tender. Add chili powder and next 7 ingredients, stirring to combine; bring to a boil. Reduce heat; simmer, covered, 30 minutes, stirring occasionally. Remove from heat, and stir in chocolate, salt, and black pepper. Yield: 12 servings (serving size: 1 cup).

CALORIES 311 (24% from fat); FAT 8.4g (sat 3.2g, mono 3.4g, poly 1g); PROTEIN 16.5g; CARB 43.9g; FIBER 12.9g; CHOL 13mg; IRON 4.1mg; SODIUM 888mg; CALC 95mg

Serve with corn bread and you've got a great meal for a casual dinner party. This chili smells so good while it's simmering that your guests will be clamoring to eat as soon as they walk in the door. The smoky chipotle chiles and Spanish chorizo combine to give this dish a kick.

Black-Eyed Pea, Kale, and Ham Soup

Tomato paste is often used in combination with other tomato products or ingredients to add depth of flavor and to give sauces a thicker and richer consistency. It's available in cans or tubes. Tubed tomato paste is convenient when recipes call for 1 tablespoon of paste at a time. You don't have to open a can just for a small amount, and the tube stores well in the refrigerator between uses.

1 tablespoon olive oil
4 ounces smoked ham, diced
1 cup diced onion
½ cup diced celery
2 garlic cloves, minced
4 cups chopped kale
1 (14.5-ounce) can petite cut diced tomatoes
2 cups frozen black-eyed peas
¾ cup water
2 (14-ounce) cans vegetable broth
2 tablespoons tomato paste
¼ teaspoon freshly ground black pepper
⅛ teaspoon cayenne pepper

1. Heat oil in a Dutch oven over medium-high heat. Add ham, onion, celery, and garlic; sauté 5 minutes or until vegetables are tender. Stir in kale and remaining ingredients; bring to a boil. Cover, reduce heat, and simmer 45 minutes or until peas are tender. Yield: 7 servings (serving size: 1 cup).

CALORIES 155 (20% from fat); FAT 3.5g (sat 0.7g, mono 1.5g, poly 0.5g); PROTEIN 9g; CARB 23.5g; FIBER 4.7g; CHOL 8mg; IRON 2mg; SODIUM 567mg; CALC 83mg

Black-eyed peas have been a staple in the South for more than three centuries. Over the years, the peas have become part of Southern folklore, and many believe that eating black-eyes on New Year's Day will bring good luck all year long. Serve this soup with some warm, golden corn bread, and luck will be on your side.

White Bean and Sausage Ragoût with Tomatoes, Kale, and Zucchini

To prepare kale, pull apart the bunch, and examine each leaf. Remove and discard any yellowed or limp portions. Wash greens in cool water, agitating with your hands. Replace water two or three times until there are no traces of dirt or grit. Lay kale flat to dry on a dish towel, or use a salad spinner to remove excess moisture. Kale leaves often have tough center veins that need to be removed. Fold the leaves in half, slice off the vein, and discard.

1 tablespoon olive oil
½ cup chopped onion
2 (4-ounce) links chicken sausage, cut into ½-inch slices
1 zucchini, quartered and cut into ½-inch slices (about 2 cups)
3 garlic cloves, peeled and crushed
6 cups chopped trimmed kale (about ½ pound)
½ cup water
¼ teaspoon salt
¼ teaspoon freshly ground black pepper
2 (16-ounce) cans cannellini beans or other white beans, rinsed and drained
1 (14.5-ounce) can diced tomatoes, undrained

1. Heat oil in a large skillet over medium-high heat. Add onion and sausage; sauté 4 minutes or until sausage is browned. Add zucchini and garlic; cook 2 minutes. Add kale and remaining ingredients; bring to a boil. Cover, reduce heat, and simmer 10 minutes or until thoroughly heated. Serve immediately. Yield: 4 servings (serving size: 1¾ cups).

CALORIES 467 (20% from fat); FAT 10.2g (sat 2.3g, mono 4.6g, poly 2.5g); PROTEIN 28.5g; CARB 71.8g; FIBER 15.4g; CHOL 42mg; IRON 8.8mg; SODIUM 764mg; CALC 370mg

Chock-full of vegetables, this colorful ragoût warms you up on a chilly winter evening.

Quick Chicken-Corn Chowder

While frozen corn kernels would speed up the prep time for this chowder, we prefer the flavor of fresh corn. Peel and discard corn silks and husks. Cut a small portion off the large end of the corn cob with a sharp knife to make an even and flat end. Stand corn cob up on flat end on a cutting board, or in the hole of a tube or Bundt pan. Cut kernels off the cob using a sawing motion.

2 tablespoons butter
¼ cup chopped onion
¼ cup chopped celery
1 jalapeño pepper, seeded and minced
2 tablespoons all-purpose flour
3 cups 2% reduced-fat milk
2 cups chopped roasted skinless, boneless chicken breast (about 2 breast halves)
1½ cups fresh or frozen corn kernels (about 3 ears)
1 teaspoon chopped fresh or ¼ teaspoon dried thyme
¼ teaspoon ground red pepper
⅛ teaspoon salt
1 (14¾-ounce) can cream-style corn
Thyme sprigs (optional)

1. Melt butter in a large Dutch oven over medium heat. Add onion, celery, and jalapeño; cook 3 minutes or until tender, stirring frequently. Add flour; cook 1 minute, stirring constantly. Stir in milk and next 6 ingredients. Bring to a boil; cook until thick (about 5 minutes), stirring frequently. Ladle soup into individual bowls. Garnish with thyme sprigs, if desired. Yield: 6 servings (serving size: about 1 cup).

CALORIES 257 (28% from fat); FAT 8.1g (sat 4.4g, mono 2.4g, poly 0.8g); PROTEIN 19.1g; CARB 28.6g; FIBER 1.9g; CHOL 52mg; IRON 0.4mg; SODIUM 668mg; CALC 165mg

Besides its hearty, filling, and comforting qualities, you can also have this soup on the table in less than 30 minutes. Its tender yellow kernels, chunky white-meat chicken, and frothy creaminess make it an all-around blue-ribbon winner.

melting pot

French Onion Soup

Although any type of onion will work, yellow onions are preferred for caramelizing. Their flavor isn't too sweet or too pungent. It's important to cut the onion into thin slices. Slice the top off the onion, leaving the root end intact. Remove the papery skin. Slice the onion in half vertically. Place halves, cut side down, on a cutting board, and cut into thin slices.

6 (1-ounce) slices French bread baguette (about ½ inch thick)
2 teaspoons butter
Cooking spray
6 cups thinly sliced onion (about 1½ pounds)
½ teaspoon sugar
⅛ teaspoon black pepper
3 tablespoons all-purpose flour
4 (14-ounce) cans fat-free, less-sodium beef broth
1 (10½-ounce) can beef consommé, undiluted
½ cup dry white wine
1 tablespoon Worcestershire sauce
¾ cup (3 ounces) grated Gruyère or Swiss cheese
⅓ cup (1⅓ ounces) grated Asiago cheese
Chopped fresh parsley (optional)

1. Preheat oven to 375°.
2. Place baguette slices on a baking sheet. Bake at 375° for 8 minutes or until lightly browned, and set aside.
3. Melt butter in a Dutch oven coated with cooking spray over medium-high heat. Add onion; sauté 5 minutes. Sprinkle onion with sugar and pepper. Reduce heat to medium-low; cook, uncovered, 30 minutes or until onion is golden, stirring frequently.
4. Sprinkle onion with flour; cook 2 minutes, stirring constantly. Add broth, consommé, and wine; bring to a boil. Reduce heat, and simmer, partially covered, 30 minutes. Remove from heat; stir in Worcestershire sauce.
5. Preheat broiler. Ladle 1½ cups soup into each of 6 ovenproof soup bowls; top each serving with 1 toast slice, 2 tablespoons Gruyère cheese, and about 1 tablespoon Asiago cheese. Place soup bowls on a large baking sheet, and broil 1 minute or until cheese melts. Sprinkle with chopped parsley, if desired. Yield: 6 servings.

CALORIES 255 (30% from fat); FAT 8.5g (sat 4.9g, mono 2.3g, poly 0.6g); PROTEIN 13.3g; CARB 31.2g; FIBER 2.6g; CHOL 25mg; IRON 1.5mg; SODIUM 895mg; CALC 258mg

Envision yourself sitting at a Parisian bistro spooning into a crusty piece of French bread baguette that's smothered with Gruyère and Asiago cheeses and surrounded by steaming broth. Now make it a reality today—minus the trip to Paris, of course. The secret to great French onion soup is to cook the onions slowly so that their natural sugars can caramelize. Don't rush it— enjoy the savory aroma in your kitchen as they simmer.

Hot and Sour Soup

Stir the broth mixture constantly with a wooden spoon while pouring the beaten egg whites into the soup. This creates the signature ribbon-like appearance of the cooked egg.

5 dried shiitake mushrooms (about ¼ ounce)
5 dried wood ear mushrooms (about ¼ ounce)
1 (32-ounce) carton fat-free, less-sodium vegetable broth
2¼ cups water, divided
1 tablespoon minced peeled fresh ginger
1 teaspoon minced garlic
¼ cup rice vinegar
1 tablespoon low-sodium soy sauce
½ to 1 teaspoon freshly ground black pepper
½ pound reduced-fat firm or extrafirm tofu, drained and cut into ¼-inch cubes
2½ tablespoons cornstarch
4 large egg whites, lightly beaten
½ cup chopped green onions
¼ cup minced fresh cilantro
1 teaspoon dark sesame oil
Chili oil (optional)

1. Place mushrooms in a medium bowl; cover with boiling water. Cover and let stand 10 minutes or until tender; drain. Thinly slice mushrooms; set aside.

2. Combine broth, 2 cups water, ginger, and garlic in a large saucepan over medium-high heat; bring to a boil. Add mushrooms. Reduce heat, and simmer 5 minutes. Add vinegar, soy sauce, pepper, and tofu; bring to a boil. Reduce heat, and simmer 5 minutes.

3. Combine remaining ¼ cup water and cornstarch, stirring with a whisk. Stir cornstarch mixture into broth mixture; bring to a boil. Reduce heat, and simmer 3 minutes or until soup thickens slightly, stirring frequently. Slowly pour egg whites into broth mixture in a steady stream, stirring constantly but gently with a wooden spoon. Remove from heat, and stir in onions, cilantro, and sesame oil. Ladle soup into individual bowls. Drizzle with chili oil, if desired. Yield: 4 servings (serving size: 1¾ cups).

CALORIES 158 (22% from fat); FAT 3.8g (sat 0.2g, mono 0g, poly 0g); PROTEIN 11.1g; CARB 20.3g; FIBER 6.5g; CHOL 0mg; IRON 1.5mg; SODIUM 770mg; CALC 44mg

A not-so-familiar Chinese proverb says to preserve the old but know the new. That's easily taken to heart with one of the great specialties of Chinese cuisine—hot and sour soup. This vegetarian version replaces the more traditional pork-based soup, helping you to eat smart and, in turn, live well.

Thai Shrimp and Chicken Soup

Coconut milk is a staple ingredient in Asian cuisine that adds rich flavor to soups and curries. Unfortunately, it's high in saturated fat. Light (or "lite") coconut milk has less fat and about a quarter of the calories of regular coconut milk. Look for canned coconut milk in the ethnic-foods section of most markets.

3 cups fat-free, less-sodium chicken broth
1 cup bottled clam juice
1 tablespoon fish sauce
2 teaspoons bottled minced garlic
1½ teaspoons bottled minced ginger
¾ teaspoon red curry paste
1 (8-ounce) package presliced mushrooms
½ pound peeled and deveined large shrimp
½ pound skinless, boneless chicken breast, cut into 1-inch pieces
1 (3-ounce) package trimmed snow peas
¼ cup fresh lime juice
2 tablespoons sugar
2 tablespoons (½-inch) sliced green onion tops
2 tablespoons chopped fresh cilantro
1 (13.5-ounce) can light coconut milk

1. Combine first 6 ingredients in a large Dutch oven, stirring with a whisk. Add mushrooms, and bring to a boil. Reduce heat, and simmer 4 minutes. Add shrimp, chicken, and snow peas; bring to a boil. Cover, reduce heat, and simmer 3 minutes.

2. Stir in lime juice and remaining ingredients. Cook 2 minutes or until thoroughly heated. Yield: 4 servings (serving size: about 2 cups).

CALORIES 262 (24% from fat); FAT 7.1g (sat 3.8g, mono 0.3g, poly 0.6g); PROTEIN 30g; CARB 18.3g; FIBER 1.8g; CHOL 121mg; IRON 3.3mg; SODIUM 973mg; CALC 64mg

Thailand, with its irresistible combination of breathtaking natural beauty, renowned hospitality, and delicious cuisine, draws more visitors each year than any other country in southeast Asia. If a trip to Bangkok isn't in your travel plans this year, you can at least bring a bit of it to your own home tonight with this tasty recipe featuring the robust flavors of garlic, ginger, mushrooms, and snow peas.

Mother's Cioppino

Crostini:
- 1 (1-pound) loaf French bread baguette, cut into 16 slices
- 1 tablespoon olive oil

Cioppino:
- 2 teaspoons olive oil
- ½ to 1 teaspoon crushed red pepper
- 4 garlic cloves, finely chopped
- 3 cups clam juice
- 1 cup water
- ½ cup finely chopped fresh parsley
- ½ teaspoon dried basil
- ¼ teaspoon dried thyme
- 1 (26-ounce) jar tomato-and-basil pasta sauce (such as Bertolli)
- 16 littleneck clams
- 16 small mussels, scrubbed and debearded
- ½ cup dry white wine
- ½ teaspoon salt
- ¼ teaspoon black pepper
- 1 pound cod or other lean white fish fillets, cut into 1-inch pieces
- ½ pound medium shrimp, peeled and deveined
- 2 cups torn spinach

1. Preheat oven to 350°.

2. To prepare crostini, place baguette slices on a large baking sheet; brush with 1 tablespoon oil. Bake at 350° for 15 minutes or until lightly browned.

3. To prepare cioppino, heat 2 teaspoons oil in a Dutch oven over medium-high heat. Add crushed red pepper and garlic; sauté 30 seconds. Stir in clam juice and next 5 ingredients. Add clams and mussels. Cover and cook 10 minutes or until shells open. Discard any unopened shells. Add wine and next 4 ingredients; simmer 5 minutes or until fish and shrimp are done. Stir in spinach. Serve with crostini. Yield: 8 servings (serving size: 1¼ cups stew and 2 crostini).

CALORIES 467 (24% from fat); FAT 12.4g (sat 1.7g, mono 4g, poly 3.6g); PROTEIN 31g; CARB 53g; FIBER 9.8g; CHOL 89mg; IRON 9.3mg; SODIUM 1,182mg; CALC 87mg

Fresh mussels are usually cooked in the shell. After scrubbing the mussels to remove any sand or dirt, you'll want to debeard them. The "beard" is the name given to the strands of tissue attached to the shell. To debeard, simply snip or pull the strands off. (Some mussels do not have beards when they are harvested.) Mussels spoil quickly after debearding, so cook them immediately.

Cioppino (chuh-PEE-noh) is a stew created by West Coast Italian immigrants who used readily available seafood along with homemade tomato and fish sauces. If you order cioppino in a San Francisco restaurant, be prepared for a hands-on encounter, especially if you have to wrestle with simmered seafood in shells in a thick red tomato sauce. We simplified the recipe with store-bought pasta sauce and clam juice. It's best served the same day it is made.

Carne con Papas

Browning meat is just that: searing the meat to a deep, rich brown color over medium-high heat. Browning also seals in the meat's flavor and juices. To get the most flavor from meat, cut it into smaller pieces to expose more surface area to be browned. When browning meat, make sure the oil is hot enough to sizzle before you add the meat. Also, cook the meat in batches rather than over-crowding the pan, and do not stir the meat too frequently.

1 teaspoon canola oil
Cooking spray
1½ pounds beef stew meat, trimmed and cut into 1-inch cubes
1½ cups chopped onion
½ cup chopped green bell pepper
½ teaspoon salt
½ teaspoon freshly ground black pepper
3 garlic cloves, minced
¼ cup water
1 teaspoon dried oregano
1 teaspoon paprika
⅛ teaspoon ground cumin
1 bay leaf, crumbled
1 (14-ounce) can low-sodium beef broth
4 cups cubed peeled baking potato (about 2 pounds)
3 tablespoons raisins
3 tablespoons coarsely chopped pimiento-stuffed olives
2 tablespoons capers

1. Heat oil in a large Dutch oven coated with cooking spray over medium-high heat. Add beef; cook 2 minutes or until browned. Add onion, bell pepper, salt, black pepper, and garlic; sauté 3 minutes. Add water and next 5 ingredients; bring to a boil. Cover, reduce heat, and cook 30 minutes.

2. Stir in potato and remaining ingredients. Cook, covered, over medium heat 20 minutes or until potato is tender, stirring occasionally. Yield: 5 servings (serving size: about 1½ cups).

CALORIES 349 (29% from fat); FAT 11.2g (sat 3.7g, mono 5.1g, poly 0.7g); PROTEIN 29.8g; CARB 32.3g; FIBER 3.2g; CHOL 85mg; IRON 4.1mg; SODIUM 673mg; CALC 43mg

This everyday meat-and-potatoes dish is best accompanied by white rice. Olives, raisins, and capers make the stew reminiscent of picadillo, a Spanish hash made from ground pork and beef or veal plus tomatoes, garlic, and onions. To streamline the preparation, chop the potatoes and olives while the beef and vegetables simmer.

Udon-Beef Noodle Bowl

Udon noodles are flat, ribbon-like Japanese wheat noodles, and they're sold dried, fresh, or pre-cooked. You're most likely to find them in Asian markets. To perfectly cook Japanese noodles and keep starchy foam from forming, use the "add water" technique. For 1 pound dried noodles, bring 4 quarts salted water to a boil; add noodles. When the water returns to a boil, stir in 1 cup cold water, and return to a boil. Repeat procedure three times. Rinse cooked noodles to remove excess starch.

8 ounces uncooked udon noodles (thick, round fresh Japanese wheat noodles) or spaghetti
1 large garlic clove, minced
½ teaspoon crushed red pepper
2 (14-ounce) cans low-sodium beef broth
3 tablespoons low-sodium soy sauce
3 tablespoons sake (rice wine) or dry sherry
1 tablespoon honey
Cooking spray
2 cups sliced shiitake mushroom caps (about 4 ounces)
½ cup thinly sliced carrot
8 ounces top round, thinly sliced
¾ cup diagonally cut green onions
1 (6-ounce) bag prewashed baby spinach

1. Cook noodles according to package directions; drain.
2. Place garlic, pepper, and broth in a large saucepan; bring to a boil. Reduce heat; simmer 10 minutes.
3. Combine soy sauce, sake, and honey in a small bowl; stir with a whisk.
4. Heat a large nonstick skillet over medium-high heat. Coat pan with cooking spray. Add mushrooms and carrot, and sauté 2 minutes. Stir in soy sauce mixture, and cook 2 minutes, stirring constantly. Add vegetable mixture to broth mixture. Stir in beef, and cook 2 minutes or until beef loses its pink color. Stir in noodles, green onions, and spinach. Serve immediately. Yield: 5 servings (serving size: about 1½ cups).

CALORIES 316 (8% from fat); FAT 2.8g (sat 0.5g, mono 0.6g, poly 0.1g); PROTEIN 20.6g; CARB 50.6g; FIBER 6.4g; CHOL 25mg; IRON 4mg; SODIUM 761mg; CALC 63mg

If you're in the mood for an Asian entrée during the week, this one falls somewhere between a soup and a noodle dish. You can eat it with chopsticks, but be sure to have spoons around to catch all of the broth.

Veal-and-Artichoke Stew with Avgolemono

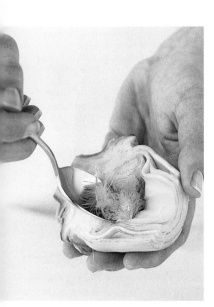

When preparing a fresh artichoke for a recipe, cut the artichoke in half lengthwise, and pull or cut out any purple spiky leaves. You'll see a fuzzy area—that's the choke. Using a sharp-edged spoon (such as a grapefruit spoon), scoop out the fuzzy choke until no hair fibers remain, and discard.

Stew:
   4 cups water, divided
   ⅔ cup fresh lemon juice (about 4 lemons), divided
   8 medium artichokes (about 10 ounces each)
   4 lemons, cut in half
2½ pounds veal round, trimmed and cut into 2-inch cubes
1½ cups coarsely chopped onion
   ½ cup dry white wine
   2 (14-ounce) cans fat-free, less-sodium chicken broth
   ½ cup chopped fresh dill
   ½ teaspoon sea salt
   ½ teaspoon freshly ground black pepper

Avgolemono:
   1 large egg
   5 tablespoons water
   2 tablespoons fresh lemon juice
1½ teaspoons cornstarch
   ¼ cup chopped fresh dill
Lemon wedges (optional)

1. To prepare stew, combine 3 cups water and ⅓ cup lemon juice in a large bowl. Working with 1 artichoke at a time, cut off stem to within 1 inch of base, and peel stem. Remove bottom leaves and tough outer leaves, and trim about 2 inches from top of artichoke. Cut artichoke in half vertically. Remove fuzzy thistle from bottom with a spoon. Trim any remaining leaves and dark green layer from base. Rub edges with a lemon half, and place artichoke halves in lemon water. Repeat procedure with remaining artichokes.
2. Heat a Dutch oven over medium-high heat, and add veal, browning on all sides. Add onion, and cook 5 minutes. Add wine and 1 can of broth; bring to a boil. Cover, reduce heat, and simmer 45 minutes.
3. Drain artichoke halves. Add artichoke halves, remaining 1 cup water, remaining ⅓ cup lemon juice, ½ cup dill, remaining 1 can of broth, salt, and pepper to pan; cover and simmer 30 minutes or until artichokes are tender. Remove veal and artichoke halves with a slotted spoon. Keep warm.
4. To prepare avgolemono, combine egg, 3 tablespoons water, and 2 tablespoons lemon juice in a medium bowl. Combine 2 tablespoons water and cornstarch in a small bowl; add to egg mixture. Add egg mixture to juices in pan. Bring to a boil; cook 5 minutes, stirring constantly with a whisk. Ladle stew into individual bowls. Serve sauce over veal and artichokes, and sprinkle with ¼ cup dill. Garnish with lemon wedges, if desired. Yield: 8 servings (serving size: 4 ounces meat, 2 artichoke halves, ¼ cup sauce, and 1½ teaspoons dill).

CALORIES 256 (12% from fat); FAT 3.4g (sat 1g, mono 1.1g, poly 0.4g); PROTEIN 37.2g; CARB 22g; FIBER 7.6g; CHOL 136mg; IRON 3.1mg; SODIUM 653mg; CALC 81mg

Calabaza and Poblano Stew

Calabaza is a large spherical or pear-shaped winter squash with a firm orange-colored flesh and a pumpkin flavor. The skin color can range from green to tan to red-orange. Butternut squash is a good substitute. If you prefer a smoother consistency, use a potato masher to break up the squash.

5 poblano chiles (about 1 pound)
1 teaspoon aniseed
1 (3-inch) cinnamon stick, broken
1 tablespoon peanut oil
3½ cups chopped onion
4 garlic cloves, minced
10 cups (2-inch) pieces peeled calabaza squash (about 3 pounds)
4 cups vegetable broth
2 cups water
3 tablespoons honey
½ teaspoon salt
6 tablespoons crema Mexicana
½ cup roasted pumpkinseed kernels

1. Preheat broiler.
2. Cut chiles in half; discard seeds and membranes. Place chile halves, skin sides up, on a foil-lined baking sheet; flatten with hand. Broil 5 minutes or until blackened. Place in a heavy-duty zip-top plastic bag; seal. Let stand 15 minutes. Peel chiles; discard skins. Chop chiles.
3. Place aniseed and cinnamon stick in a spice or coffee grinder; process until finely ground.
4. Heat oil in a large Dutch oven over medium-high heat. Add onion; sauté 5 minutes or until browned. Add garlic; sauté 1 minute. Add cinnamon mixture to pan; sauté 1 minute. Add chopped chiles, squash, broth, water, honey, and salt; bring to a boil. Reduce heat, and simmer 30 minutes or until squash is tender.
5. Ladle stew into individual bowls. Drizzle each serving with crema Mexicana, and sprinkle with pumpkinseeds. Yield: 8 servings (serving size: 1½ cups stew, about 2 teaspoons crema Mexicana, and 1 tablespoon pumpkinseeds).

CALORIES 266 (35% from fat); FAT 10.4g (sat 2.6g, mono 2.7g, poly 3.4g); PROTEIN 9g; CARB 40.7g; FIBER 8.4g; CHOL 8mg; IRON 4mg; SODIUM 669mg; CALC 118mg

Redolent with honey, cinnamon, and aniseed, this stew highlights the exotic flavors that are typically associated with European cuisine but are also commonly used in Mexico. Crema Mexicana, which is similar to crème fraîche but has a thinner consistency and a sweeter flavor, helps to tone down the spiciness of the stew.

Posole

Tomatillos, a close cousin to tomatoes, have a tart flavor that make Mexican green sauces so distinct. They are about the size of a large cherry tomato, and they have a papery outer skin and a white inside that is meatier than a tomato. Hominy is dried corn kernels that have been treated with an alkali of some kind. This process removes the germ and the hard outer hull from the kernels, making them more palatable, easier to digest, and easier to process.

1 pound tomatillos
6 cups Brown Chicken Stock (page 138) or fat-free, less-sodium chicken broth
2 cups chopped onion
3 pounds bone-in chicken breast halves, skinned
4 garlic cloves, chopped
2 jalapeño peppers, seeded and quartered
1 (30-ounce) can white hominy, drained
1 teaspoon salt
½ cup chopped fresh cilantro
¼ cup reduced-fat sour cream
8 lime wedges

1. Discard husks and stems from tomatillos. Cook tomatillos in boiling water 10 minutes or until tender; drain. Place in a blender; process until smooth.
2. Place stock and next 5 ingredients in a large stockpot; bring to a boil. Cover, reduce heat, and simmer 35 minutes or until chicken is done. Remove chicken from pot. Stir in puréed tomatillos and salt, and cook 5 minutes or until heated. Remove chicken from bones; shred. Stir in chicken. Ladle soup into individual bowls; serve with cilantro, sour cream, and lime wedges. Yield: 8 servings (serving size: 1½ cups soup, 1 tablespoon cilantro, 1½ teaspoons sour cream, and 1 lime wedge).

(Totals include Brown Chicken Stock) CALORIES 233 (16% from fat); FAT 4.1g (sat 1.3g, mono 0.7g, poly 0.8g); PROTEIN 31.8g; CARB 19.4g; FIBER 4g; CHOL 79mg; IRON 1.8mg; SODIUM 548mg; CALC 46mg

Posole (poh-SOH-leh) is a thick, hearty soup from the Pacific Coast region of Mexico. It features chicken broth, fluffy white hominy, chopped onions, zesty jalapeño peppers, and vibrant green cilantro. It's traditionally served as a main course during the Christmas season. A lime garnish adds color and a festive look to your presentation.

Jamaican Chicken Stew

Canned beans are more convenient than dried beans. For the best results, rinse thoroughly with tap water before using, and drain in a colander. Rinsing canned beans gets rid of the thick liquid in the can and reduces the sodium by 40 percent.

1 cup uncooked long-grain rice
2 teaspoons olive oil
1 cup chopped onion
1 large garlic clove, minced
1 pound skinless, boneless chicken breast, cut into bite-sized pieces
1 teaspoon curry powder
1 teaspoon dried thyme
½ teaspoon ground allspice
½ teaspoon crushed red pepper
½ teaspoon cracked black pepper
¼ cup dry red wine
2 tablespoons capers
1 (15-ounce) can black beans, rinsed and drained
1 (14.5-ounce) can diced tomatoes, undrained
Cilantro sprigs (optional)

1. Prepare rice according to package directions, omitting salt and fat. Keep warm.

2. Heat oil in a large nonstick skillet over medium-high heat. Add onion and garlic, and sauté 3 minutes or until tender. Combine chicken and next 5 ingredients. Add chicken mixture to pan; sauté 4 minutes. Stir in wine, capers, beans, and tomatoes. Cover, reduce heat, and simmer 10 minutes or until tender. Spoon rice into individual bowls; ladle stew over rice. Garnish with cilantro sprigs, if desired. Yield: 4 servings (serving size: 1½ cups stew and ¾ cup rice).

CALORIES 465 (10% from fat); FAT 5g (sat 1g, mono 2.2g, poly 1g); PROTEIN 38.5g; CARB 66g; FIBER 5.9g; CHOL 66mg; IRON 6mg; SODIUM 799mg; CALC 101mg

This classic Jamaican stew will usher you to the island in spirit and have you saying "Yah mon!" before your second bite. Add jalapeño-style corn bread and pineapple sorbet for a simple weeknight supper.

Turkey Vatapa

Before mincing, gingerroot should be peeled with a vegetable peeler or paring knife. Like garlic, you can mince it with a sharp knife by cutting it into tiny irregular pieces or pressing it with a garlic press.

1 teaspoon peanut or canola oil
½ cup finely chopped onion
3 garlic cloves, minced
1 tablespoon minced peeled fresh ginger
1 jalapeño pepper, minced
1 cup water
1 (28-ounce) can no salt–added diced tomatoes, undrained
1 (12-ounce) can light beer
¼ cup unsalted, dry-roasted peanuts
3 cups chopped cooked turkey or chicken
½ cup light coconut milk
½ cup finely chopped fresh parsley
½ cup finely chopped fresh cilantro
1 tablespoon fresh lime juice
½ teaspoon salt
½ teaspoon black pepper
Cilantro sprigs (optional)

1. Heat oil in a Dutch oven over medium-high heat. Add onion and garlic; sauté 2 minutes. Add ginger and jalapeño; sauté 30 seconds. Stir in water, tomatoes, and beer; bring to a boil. Cover, reduce heat, and simmer 20 minutes.

2. Place peanuts in a spice or coffee grinder, and process until finely ground. Add ground peanuts, chopped turkey, and coconut milk to pan, stirring to combine. Increase heat to medium. Bring mixture to a simmer, and cook 5 minutes, stirring occasionally. Stir in chopped parsley, chopped cilantro, lime juice, salt, and black pepper. Ladle stew into individual bowls. Garnish with cilantro sprigs, if desired. Yield: 6 servings (serving size: 1⅓ cups).

CALORIES 195 (30% from fat); FAT 6.4g (sat 1.8g, mono 2.3g, poly 1.7g); PROTEIN 19.9g; CARB 11.8g; FIBER 3.3g; CHOL 56mg; IRON 2.3mg; SODIUM 301mg; CALC 55mg

Vatapa is a rustic Brazilian stew, a fiery blend with beer, coconut milk, and ground peanuts as its base. Made with leftover holiday turkey or rotisserie chicken, it's a snap to prepare. Vatapa can be made up to two days in advance; keep it covered in the refrigerator. It will thicken as it sits; just add a little water. Seed the jalapeño pepper to tame its heat.

all about
Soup

Soup is the true melting pot of all the world's best ingredients. And at *Cooking Light*, we've found that soup can be one of the best introductions to the genius and chemistry of cooking.

Soup is basic. Its techniques are classic. And by blending time-honored skills such as sautéing, caramelizing, deglazing, and thickening, you can have dinner on the table without feeling overwhelmed or intimidated. Just remember, it all starts with the stock or broth.

Stocks

The key to a great soup is a homemade stock. The slow simmering of meats, vegetables, herbs, and spices produces a flavorful liquid—the foundation for soup. Making your own stock is advantageous to healthy cooking. It allows you to create intense natural flavor while keeping the amount of sodium very low.

Broths

A broth is basically made from the same ingredients as a stock. However, broth is cooked in less time, isn't as intensely flavored, and often contains more sodium. Broths may be used in place of stock when you are short on time; our Test Kitchens often use broths for that reason.

Commercial Products

Homemade stocks and broths are superior to commercial products, but they're not always practical. In those cases, we suggest using commercial products. The flavor and the amounts of sodium and fat will vary among brands. Note the comparisons in the chart below.

Stock Versus Broth Nutritional Comparisons

Here's how homemade and commercial stocks and broths compare nutritionally.

Ingredient (1 cup)	Calories	Fat	Sodium
Homemade beef stock	8	0.3g	9mg
Regular commercial beef stock	15	1g	890mg
*Less-sodium beef broth	15	1g	440mg
Homemade white chicken stock	28	0.8g	18mg
Regular commercial chicken stock	10	0.5g	960mg
*Fat-free, less-sodium chicken broth	15	0g	570mg
Homemade vegetable stock	8	0.1g	2mg
*Less-sodium vegetable broth	15	0g	570mg

Cooking Light Test Kitchens prefer to use Swanson canned broths in recipes.

Essential Techniques for Making Stocks

Master the art of making stocks with this step-by-step guide.

White Chicken Stock

White stock is best to use when you need a mild flavor that won't overpower delicate ingredients, and it's also good to keep in the freezer for other recipes. Its light color suits risotto, mashed potatoes, and cream soups. White stock is prepared entirely on the stovetop.

½ teaspoon black peppercorns
10 parsley sprigs
8 thyme sprigs
3 celery stalks, cut into 2-inch-thick pieces
3 bay leaves
2 medium onions, peeled and quartered
2 carrots, cut into 2-inch-thick pieces
2 garlic cloves, crushed
6 pounds chicken pieces
16 cups cold water

1. Place first 8 ingredients in an 8-quart stockpot; add chicken and water. Bring mixture to a boil over medium heat. Reduce heat, and simmer, uncovered, 3 hours. Strain stock through a fine sieve into a large bowl. Reserve chicken for another use; discard remaining solids. Cover and chill stock 8 hours. Skim solidified fat from surface of stock; discard fat. Yield: 10 cups (serving size: 1 cup).

CALORIES 28 (26% from fat); FAT 0.8g (sat 0.2g, mono 0.3g, poly 0.2g); PROTEIN 4.7g; CARB 0.4g; FIBER 0.1g; CHOL 15mg; IRON 0.3mg; SODIUM 18mg; CALC 4mg

1. Prepare the ingredients. Peel and quarter the onions. Rinse, peel, and trim the carrots and celery. This will result in a cleaner, less-cloudy stock and will help infuse the stock with the flavor of the vegetables.

2. Start with cold water. Add only enough cold water to barely cover the ingredients in the pot. Too much water will dilute the stock's flavor. Be sure the

water is cold. Pouring hot water over chicken or meat will release specks of protein that will make the stock cloudy.
3. Don't add salt. The stock will concentrate during cooking, so it doesn't need salt. Instead, add the salt to the final soup recipe so that you can control the sodium.

4. Simmer and skim. As soon as the water in the stockpot comes to a boil, reduce the heat to a simmer. Simmering means your liquid is not quite boiling, but there should be noticeable small bubbles that continually rise to the surface. You will also notice a gray foam rising to the surface of the stock. Gently remove and discard this foam with a spoon, ladle, or skimmer. If you don't remove the foam, it will eventually reincorporate into the stock, making it cloudy and impeding the taste. Continue to allow the stock to simmer for several hours to develop a rich flavor.

5. Strain. Place a fine sieve over a large bowl or pot in the sink. Start by straining the stock in batches, transferring it from the pot to the sieve with a ladle until the stockpot is light enough to lift.

6. Remove the fat. Return the strained stock to the stockpot, and place it in the refrigerator. If the stockpot doesn't fit in the refrigerator, divide the stock among a few smaller vessels. As the stock chills, the fat will solidify on top, making it easy to remove.

7. Reduce. Once the fat is removed, the stock is ready to use. However, it's a good idea to reduce all of it right away to concentrate the flavors and save on storage space. Bring the stock to a simmer again, and let it reduce by half the volume.

8. Store. Cool up to 4 quarts of stock in the stockpot in the refrigerator. Reduced stock takes on the consistency of gelatin after it has chilled, making it easy to handle. Just keep it in a tub, and spoon it out as needed. Stock will keep in the refrigerator up to a week and in the freezer up to 3 months. Just pour the stock into airtight containers, filling them three-fourths full to allow room for the liquid to expand as it freezes. Freeze smaller amounts in ice-cube trays; then remove the cubes from the trays, and store them in zip-top freezer bags.

No Time to Chill

Chilling the stock overnight makes degreasing a cinch because the fat solidifies on top. But you can also proceed with a recipe right after making the stock. Our favorite methods involve either a zip-top plastic bag or a fat separator cup. The cup is made of inexpensive plastic or glass and has a spout at the base. When you pour out the stock, the fat floating on the top stays behind. The bag works similarly. Pour stock into bag; and let stand 10 minutes (fat will rise to the top). Seal bag; carefully snip off 1 bottom corner of bag. Drain stock into a container, stopping before fat layer reaches opening; discard fat.

How to Make Brown Chicken Stock

Brown stock has deeper flavor than white stock, and the procedure involves caramelizing chicken and vegetables in the oven for half the cooking time and then putting them in a stockpot to simmer during the second half of cooking.

1. Roasting the vegetables and chicken until browned creates a deep, rich caramelized flavor.

2. The browned bits from the pan add even more flavor. Deglaze the pan by adding water and scraping up the bits.

3. Simmer the stock ingredients for 1½ hours. Then strain through a fine sieve.

4. Skim the fat from the stock after the stock has chilled 8 hours or overnight.

Brown Chicken Stock

Use a pan large enough to roast the chicken and all of the vegetables in a single layer. If the pan is too small, the chicken won't brown properly.

¼ pound fennel stalks, cut into
    2-inch-thick pieces
3 carrots, cut into 2-inch-thick pieces
1 celery stalk, cut into 2-inch-thick
    pieces
1 medium onion, peeled and
    quartered
6 pounds chicken pieces
½ teaspoon black peppercorns
6 parsley sprigs
5 thyme sprigs
2 bay leaves
16 cups cold water, divided

1. Preheat oven to 400°.
2. Arrange first 4 ingredients in bottom of a broiler or roasting pan; top with chicken. Bake at 400° for 1½ hours; turn chicken once every 30 minutes (chicken and vegetables should be very brown).
3. Place peppercorns, parsley, thyme, and bay leaves in an 8-quart stockpot. Remove vegetables and chicken from broiler pan; place in stockpot. Discard drippings from broiler pan, leaving browned bits. Place broiler pan on stovetop; add 4 cups water. Bring to a

boil over medium-high heat. Reduce heat; simmer 10 minutes, scraping pan to loosen browned bits.

4. Pour contents of pan into stockpot. Add remaining 12 cups water; bring to a boil over medium-high heat. Reduce heat; simmer 1½ hours.

5. Strain stock through a fine sieve into a large bowl. Reserve chicken for another use; discard remaining solids. Cover and chill stock 8 hours. Skim solidified fat from surface of stock; discard fat. Yield: 10 cups (serving size: 1 cup).

CALORIES 31 (32% from fat); FAT 1.1g (sat 0.3g, mono 0.4g, poly 0.2g); PROTEIN 4.7g; CARB 0.4g; FIBER 0.1g; CHOL 15mg; IRON 0.3mg; SODIUM 19mg; CALC 4mg

Vegetable Stock

This all-purpose vegetable stock has woodsy undertones. You can improvise with your choice of vegetables, but avoid bitter ones, which can compete with the flavors of the finished dish.

12 cups water
 1 (8-ounce) package mushrooms, sliced
 1 cup chopped onion
¾ cup chopped carrot
½ cup coarsely chopped celery
½ cup chopped parsnip
 2 bay leaves
 2 thyme sprigs
 1 whole garlic head, halved

1. Combine all ingredients in a Dutch oven; bring to a boil. Reduce heat, and simmer until reduced to 6 cups (about 1 hour). Strain stock through a fine sieve into a large bowl; discard solids. Refrigerate leftover stock in an airtight container for up to 1 week, or freeze for up to 3 months. Yield: 6 cups (serving size: 1 cup).

CALORIES 8 (11% from fat); FAT 0.1g (sat 0g, mono 0g, poly 0.1g); PROTEIN 0.3g; CARB 1.7g; FIBER 0.3g; CHOL 0mg; IRON 0.1mg; SODIUM 2mg; CALC 7mg

Beef Stock

Beef stock—made from beef and veal bones—is the basis of many classic European sauces. It makes quick, light, deeply flavored pan sauces.

3½ pounds meaty beef bones (such as oxtail)
 3 cups coarsely chopped celery
1½ cups chopped carrot (about ¾ pound)
 2 tablespoons tomato paste
 3 medium onions, peeled and halved (about 1½ pounds)
20 cups water

1. Preheat oven to 400°.
2. Arrange bones in an even layer in a shallow roasting pan. Bake at 400° for 45 minutes or until browned.
3. Transfer bones to an 8-quart stockpot. Add celery, carrot, tomato paste, and onions to pot; stir well to combine. Pour water over mixture; bring mixture to a simmer. Reduce heat, and simmer 5 hours, skimming surface occasionally.
4. Strain stock through a fine sieve into a large bowl; discard solids. Cool stock to room temperature. Cover and chill stock 8 to 24 hours. Skim solidified fat from surface; discard. Refrigerate remaining stock in an airtight container for up to 1 week, or freeze for up to 3 months. Yield: 10 cups (serving size: 1 cup).

CALORIES 8 (31% from fat); FAT 0.3g (sat 0.1g, mono 0.1g, poly 0g); PROTEIN 0.7g; CARB 0.7g; FIBER 0.1g; CHOL 2mg; IRON 0.1mg; SODIUM 9mg; CALC 4mg

Arrange bones in an even layer in a shallow roasting pan. Bake at 400° for 45 minutes or until browned.

Reduce heat, and simmer 5 hours, skimming surface occasionally to remove the foam.

Essential Techniques for Making Soup

Use these cooking tips and techniques as a quick reference when making soup.

1. Sauté. Sautéing vegetables fills your home with a wonderful aroma. Slowly cook a combination of vegetables (such as onions, garlic, carrots, and celery) plus herbs and spices in a small amount of fat (butter, oil, or even bacon drippings for a salty, smoky flavor) until the vegetables are tender. It's a good idea to pay close attention and to stir constantly with a wooden spoon to keep the food from burning. The goal is to cook the vegetables until they're tender. If the vegetables burn, they may add a bitter, undesirable flavor to the soup. It's much better to start over at this point in the recipe rather than compromising the flavor of the whole pot of soup.

2. Caramelize and brown. Vegetables contain natural sugars. As you slowly cook them, these sugars are released and begin to turn the vegetables brown (or caramelize them). This is different from scorching or burning. As the vegetables brown, they begin to release rich flavors. It's the blending of these flavors that's the foundation of soups.

Recipes that call for meat often direct you to brown the meat before continuing with the recipe. It's important to cook the meat in small batches so that it gets a nice brown color on all sides. This browning process contributes deep flavor to the soup. Don't rush and try to cook all of the meat at one time. If you do, the meat will steam rather than brown, and you won't have the rich flavor or brown color that is so important to the overall taste and appearance of the soup.

3. Deglaze. It's important not to leave any concentrated flavor in the bottom of a skillet or pan. Add a small amount of liquid—stock, broth, water, wine, or a combination—to loosen the browned bits of caramelized food. These browned bits contribute greatly to the flavor of the soup. Besides that, leaving the browned bits on the bottom of the pan may cause the soup or stew to stick, which will cause burning.

4. Simmer. Now that you have the flavor base for your soup, it's time to add the remaining ingredients. Begin with those that have to cook the longest, such as beans, rice, potatoes, and the remaining liquid. Cover the pot, and cook over low heat until done. Stir the soup occasionally to make sure that nothing sticks to the bottom of the pan.

5. Thicken. Some soups have a clear, thin broth. Others, such as chowders and cream soups, are thick and creamy.

To reduce the fat but maintain the flavor and texture of a cream soup, combine a small amount of cream, evaporated skim milk, or reduced-fat milk with flour, and stir this mixture into the soup near the end of the cooking time. It is important to bring the soup back to a boil, reduce the heat, and cook, stirring occasionally, at least 10 to 15 minutes or until thick. Otherwise, the soup may taste like flour and be too thin. For bean, lentil, or vegetable soups, remove about 1 cup of the soup near the end of the cooking time. Purée it in a blender or mash it with a fork or potato masher, and stir it back into the soup.

Freezing Soups

To freeze. Pour soup into an airtight container, leaving enough room for expansion (usually an inch or two at the top of the container).

To reheat. Thaw completely in the refrigerator; then place the contents in a saucepan over low heat. Add a little extra water or broth if the soup seems too thick. **Soups that don't freeze well.** Most soups can be frozen, but creamy soups such as bisques and chowders that contain cream or potato don't freeze well. They tend to taste grainy when thawed and reheated. Cold fruit soups also do not freeze well. Their delicate, fresh flavor is lost when thawed. If a soup contains rice, it is best to have the rice only partially cooked upon freezing; you can complete the cooking time for the rice when reheating.

How to Dress Up Soup with Style

1. For casual meals, serve soup right from the pot. Or for casual entertaining, use soup tureens or shiny copper pots.

2. Use your imagination when choosing individual serving bowls. Deep bowls and mugs are good for chunky soups. Wide-rimmed, shallow bowls are ideal for smooth, creamy soups that only need a simple garnish, or for clear broth soups where the broth itself creates its own beauty.

3. Consider nontraditional serving dishes such as a cup and saucer for a first-course soup, or assorted stemware for a dessert soup.

4. To keep the soup from cooling too quickly, rinse the serving bowls with hot water just before ladling. For chilled soups, place the empty bowls in the refrigerator about 30 minutes before filling.

5. Use simple garnishes, such as lemon or lime wedges or grated, shredded, or shaved cheeses. Sometimes the ingredients used in the recipe can be used to garnish the soup as well as enhancing flavor and texture.

6. If the soup calls for fresh herbs, set aside a few extra sprigs before you begin. You may use the sprigs later as a garnish, or you could chop a little extra to scatter over the soup before serving.

7. For cream or puréed soups, garnish with whole, thinly sliced, or chopped vegetables.

8. A dollop of low-fat sour cream or yogurt can tame the heat and add the finishing touch to a bowl of spicy soup. Or it can also be swirled into a creamy soup for a decorative presentation.

9. Sprinkle soup with homemade or store-bought croutons or fresh tortillas cut into chips or strips. Or simply lay a breadstick across the rim of the soup bowl.

10. Mound rice or pasta in the center of a bowl (or even off-center), and ladle the soup around it, taking care not to completely cover the rice or pasta.

Subject Index

Recipe Index